PASSIONATE ABOUT
Baking

EBURY PRESS

USA | Canada | UK | Ireland | Australia
New Zealand | India | South Africa | China | Singapore

Ebury Press is part of the Penguin Random House group of companies
whose addresses can be found at global.penguinrandomhouse.com

Published by Penguin Random House India Pvt. Ltd
4th Floor, Capital Tower 1, MG Road,
Gurugram 122 002, Haryana, India

First published in Ebury Press by Penguin Random House India 2021

Copyright © Deeba Rajpal 2021

ISBN 9780143449928

Book and design layout: Meher Rajpal

Typeset in Minion Pro by Manipal Technologies Limited, Manipal
Printed at Aarvee Promotions, India

www.penguin.co.in

PASSIONATE ABOUT
Baking

Picture-Perfect, Easy and
Indulgent Chocolate Recipes to Make at Home

DEEBA RAJPAL

EBURY
PRESS

An imprint of Penguin Random House

To the best furries in the world, Coco and Bambi,
who sat by me every minute of every recipe in this book,
knowing pretty well no chocolate would ever come their way.

Contents

Foreword

Having followed Deeba Rajpal's work on social media for a few years now, I have been struck with how effortless her baking seems.

Don't have baking powder? Simple, just use X ingredient and you're good to go. Don't want to use egg in your cake? No problem, Y ingredient will do the job just as efficiently. Want less flour/more nut powder/more local flavours/less fuss? Leave it to Rajpal.

She has found the solution to all your individual needs, and what's more, she communicates it to you in the most direct way possible, eliminating the jargon that terrifies most first-time bakers.

My nieces and nephews all think that I'm a cake and cookie fairy, thanks to the edible gifts that emanate from my (embarrassingly amateur) oven. I don't let on that it is actually Deeba Rajpal they should be thanking for the largesse!

Marryam H. Reshii
Writer & Food Critic

Introduction

I never imagined I would write a cookbook, forget keep a blog alive for so long. On the contrary, in more ways than one, I think the blog kept me 'alive', motivating me to think outside of the box and push my boundaries! The journey has been memorable and a huge learning experience. I have read a few rather daunting cookbooks which made me wonder at times if my approach was far too simple, almost a no-brainer! Was I missing something?

As the years passed, as my interactions on social media grew, I realized that whatever I was doing was just as good. There were a number of baking and dessert enthusiasts who found that my way worked for them time and again. This encouraged me to create more, share more and find confidence in what I enjoyed creating the most: desserts!

You Might Ask, Why Desserts?

To be honest, I don't have a sweet tooth at all. The most I will bend for is bittersweet chocolate and coffee—those two are my greatest indulgence. I bake for others, for the happiness it gives them, for the joy it gives me to share, virtually and otherwise. Also, for the joy that styling and shooting gives me—so much to look forward to, so much to play around with, so much to fill my days.

Seasons, textures, moods, culture, colours, light, nature, produce, people, stories, old cities, heritage, vintage collectibles—I find inspiration everywhere. I have an innate desire to capture everything in frame, something my sadly overburdened hard drives and cell phone will tell you if they could talk. They groan under the weight of my obsession, much like all the storage at home. Stuffed to the gills with props of every kind—ceramic, stone, wood, metal. You name it, I have it. Hopefully this book will showcase a little bit of all my interests, including food styling and photography.

My journey into baking took a turn the day I realized that most of what I was doing consisted of empty calories. That was my eureka moment, a wake-up call, a new way forward. From then on, I became more conscious of ingredients like plain flour or all-purpose flour and refined sugars. Every ingredient I used had to make itself worthwhile. I am in no way an extremist; I have just balanced myself better. I understand that it's a matter of playing with the palate, developing heartier, more wholesome desserts, and understanding how healthy can be delicious so easily.

I feel fortunate to have been associated with several brands as I went along. That part of my journey made me grow, think and create differently. It's always nice to offer value to brands you believe in, and it's a great way to develop your creative process. You'll read about California Walnuts India and Cadbury in a few of my recipes, to mention a couple here.

It's not my business to tell others what to do, but I feel good when I share my ideas. It's quite a special feeling when they are received so well, and my eureka moments accepted so hungrily! I now have a whole band of folk who walk with me saying,

'Hey, made your brownies, and the kids couldn't even tell they were made with regular wholewheat flour or atta.'
Or, 'Good heavens, why didn't someone tell me ghee and baking go so well together?'
Also, 'Garam masala in pudding? Made it thrice over the weekend. Just can't get enough!'

The bottom line: I'm fearless while baking. For me, it isn't a daunting science. Much like with photography, I am technically quite mediocre, but I operate with my heart. Hopefully, the images I have styled and shot for the book reflect that piece of heart. So whether it is baking, cooking, styling or shooting, I follow few rules. For me, the process is intuitive and I am always happy to experiment. **What If?** is an important part of my journey, and you will find 'What If?' boxes at the base of a few recipes. If something doesn't work out, it teaches me something; in my humble opinion, that's the best way to learn. And because I know I use good ingredients, I can always upcycle my failures. An Eton Mess wasn't born out of nothing, and trifles are a thing, right?

Come, dive right into my book and enjoy it. Tread carefully, but don't be scared. Read the recipe through, make notes if you like, ask questions, seek answers. How else will we find joy in the mundane?

I'll end with lines from an email I recently received:

I had to connect with you for the immense delight your baking endeavours give me. From the baking process, the ingredients, your presentation verbally and visually, everything touches my senses and soul.
When I see your posts on the blog, I am forced to say this: 'What! You too? I thought I was the only one.'

Reading such words just puts everything in a happy place. Makes it real! Thank you all for being part of my journey. I found the courage to write a book because of you!

My Pantry Essentials

If you like making desserts, chances are that you are already quite well-equipped. Here's a list of staples I always have on hand. What you make is a result of the quality of ingredients you use, so stock up well!

CHOCOLATE

Pure, unsweetened chocolate is often called couverture or baking chocolate, and is primarily made up of cocoa solids and cocoa butter in different proportions. The percentage of chocolate indicates the intensity of flavour. The higher the percentage, the less sweet it is, with a more intense chocolate flavour. While unsweetened chocolate is very bitter and finds use in commercial baking, a popular choice for home use is dark or bittersweet, where the percentage can vary from 54% to 85%. It's a matter of choice, and you could well use a semi-sweet or milk chocolate that has less intensity.

I don't use compound chocolate since it contains trans fats, which means the benefits of a good chocolate are lost. Also, the flavour profile of compound chocolate is far inferior to couverture chocolate. It is said that dark chocolate is a superfood packed with antioxidants and flavonoids, and definitely good for you. I'll go with that!

I normally use a range of 54–80% couverture chocolate, and usually source it from **www.bakerykart.com**.

Bittersweet Chocolate (70.5–80% Chocolate): If bittersweet is difficult to source, then use dark chocolate and adjust the sweetness accordingly. Lindt 75–80% or Amul Bitter Intense Chocolate might be a good substitute.

Dark Chocolate (54–70% Chocolate): It's a good choice, one which balances taste and cost beautifully! If you are struggling to source a good dark baking chocolate, then your next best bet might be Amul Single-Origin Dark Chocolate or Lindt Dark Chocolate.

White Chocolate: I use the Callebaut W2 white couverture. A reasonably good substitute is a Lindt white, or maybe an Amul white.

Chocolate Chips: I most often use Callebaut couverture callets, which are made of tempered chocolate and melt easily. They make an excellent ganache, though I also use them as add-ins for my cookies and loaves where chocolate chips are required. Just makes it easier to manage my stock. I also use Nestle Toll House and Ghirardelli chocolate chips. You could chop up a bar or slab of chocolate if you can't source chocolate chips.

Cocoa Powder: The brands I use are Van Houten, All Things Chocolate, Callebaut, Hershey's and Cacao Berry.

Cocoa Nibs: These are made from crushed cocoa beans and are said to be packed with nutrients. They offer great texture and flavour profile to desserts, granola, etc. Call them natural chocolate chips, I find the slight edgy bitterness and depth of taste quite addictive. They also add magic as a quick garnish if you need to pretty up dessert in a hurry!

*(**Note:** For vegan desserts, vegan baking chocolates are also available in the market.)*

SWEETENERS

I use most sugars interchangeably, depending on what I have on hand. It might not be the ideal thing to do, but it works just fine for me.

Sugar: Castor sugar or normal everyday sugar, also referred to as crystal, granulated, maybe white sugar.

Brown Sugar: Use a good demerara or muscovado.

Icing Sugar: Often used to make a whipped cream or frosting, icing sugar is available as a packaged product. Powder white sugar fine to make icing sugar if you need an emergency fix. A coffee grinder or dry grinder should do the trick.

Vanilla Sugar: I usually have jars of sugar with vanilla beans tucked in hiding in my pantry, building flavour over weeks. You'll find an easy recipe in the 'Basics to Bottles' chapter at the end of the book.

Coconut Sugar: Once I discovered coconut sugar, I just couldn't stop using it! It adds deep, almost caramel tones and beautiful character to dessert. An easy substitute would be brown sugar.

Jaggery Powder/Gur: An unrefined sugar quintessential to Indian cuisine, gur is moist and deep in flavour, adding beautiful earthy notes to dessert. While sugar is sugar, jaggery is said to be slightly more nutritious than refined white sugar. In recipes where gur is mentioned, I use organic jaggery powder which is fairly easily available. An easy substitute would be brown sugar.

Honey: Substitute with maple syrup (a good vegan alternative), if required.

DAIRY

Good-quality dairy products make food taste good. Look for quality brands, or brands you grew up with and trust. Often, your taste buds prefer one brand over another, so go with that. Most dairy products are very easily available in India, and that's a blessing.

Unsalted Butter: Simple unsalted white butter, either home-made or store-bought. Most brands now do 100 g or 500 g packs of unsalted butter that keep well in the fridge. 100 g packages are more convenient because you can easily use half for a 50 g amount if required. I use either home-made white butter, or else Amul, Gopala, Mother Dairy, etc.

Salted Butter: Can be used interchangeably with unsalted butter. Just skip adding salt if the recipe calls for unsalted butter.

Clarified Butter/Ghee: One of my most used ingredients from this group, I prefer clarified butter/ghee over normal butter in baking because it offers delightful deep notes to the bake, tastes great and keeps well at room temperature. It's a staple in the Indian kitchen. I still remember the spoonfuls I used to sneak into my mouth as a kid; that taste of home-made ghee in winter is hard to forget.

It surprises a lot of my readers to see me use ghee in baking, sweet desserts, and in cakes and cookies. Bear with me. Give it a shot at least once. If you aren't smitten, there's always butter!

*(**Note:** Clarified butter and ghee are almost similar and can be used interchangeably.)*

Buttermilk: Cultured buttermilk is easily available in the local markets in India. Look for plain chaach or chaas sold by major dairy brands like Amul, Mother Dairy, etc. There's a very simple home-made substitute in the 'Basics to Bottles' chapter at the end of the book.

Yogurt: Packaged yogurt is thicker than home-made yogurt. If all you have is home-made yogurt, consider putting it in a cheesecloth-lined sieve and standing it over a bowl in the fridge to get rid of excess whey. The whey can be used in smoothies, lassi and curries.

Greek Yogurt: This is a thicker and protein-dense version of normal yogurt. The best thing that happened to yogurt and the best yogurt that happened to baking! Greek yogurt isn't that easily available and is a bit heavy on the wallet. Epigamia makes good Greek yogurt. Hung yogurt with the excess whey removed can be used as a substitute.

Cream: I use Amul Fresh cream (20% fat) in all my recipes, unless specified otherwise.

Mascarpone: This soft, sweet cheese is easily available in local stores by brands like Mooz, Flanders, D'lecta, etc. If you feel a little adventurous, you can make it at home quite easily. I have a recipe on the blog, **www.passionateaboutbaking.com**.

Cream Cheese: I use local brands like D'lecta, Flanders and Mooz, sometimes Britannia. They all work reasonably well.

NON-DAIRY

Neutral Oil: Sunflower or light olive oil—anything that doesn't have overpowering taste notes works well.

Coconut Milk: One of my most-used non-dairy ingredients, coconut milk pairs beautifully with chocolate. It adds creaminess without heaviness and is a great vegan alternative. Real Thai and Urban Platter are good brands.

FLOUR

Experimenting with wholegrain flour changed the way I baked forever. Hopefully, my recipes will begin to change that for you too. I enjoy using a mix of flours in my baking, and they include all sorts, from all-purpose to wholegrain flours. I began using the hashtag **#makehalfyourgrainswhole** to constantly remind me of how I changed what I do every day!

Wholewheat Flour: Also known as atta, this is the flour I use most often in my baking. It's the normal flour/atta that we use for chapatis. I use Aashirwad Select. I've tried the more specialized heirloom flours and organic flours and those work well too. The only disadvantage is that they need better storage conditions and tend to go rancid pretty quick. If you're looking to bring about a small change in the way you bake, possibly begin with the wholewheat flour you use every day, your pantry staple.

All-Purpose Flour/Plain Flour: It's a standard, easily available ingredient that you get at every corner store. Maida is the same as all-purpose flour. This is *not* the same as self-raising flour.

Oat Flour: A gluten-free flour, simply made by grinding quick cooking oats at home in a dry grinder, oat flour is available in stores too.

Gram Flour/Besan: A gluten-free ingredient which I've just begun experimenting with while baking.

Buckwheat Flour/Kuttu ka Atta: I buy small amounts and store it in the freezer since it tends to go rancid pretty quickly. I use it often in both sweet and savoury bakes.

Quinoa Flour: Another gluten-free alternative; local brands are now easily available. This flour tends to go rancid pretty soon, so it's best stored in a cool place or in the fridge.

LEAVENERS

Baking Powder: A quintessential baking ingredient, but do always make sure the batch is fresh. A quick freshness test is to drop 1 tsp into ⅓ cup of hot water. If it bubbles, it's fresh. Baking soda and baking powder are *not* interchangeable since both work differently when combined with different ingredients in recipes.

Baking soda: Also called 'meetha soda' which you might add to cook chhole or chickpeas, it's important to have a fresh batch on hand. A quick freshness test is to drop ¼ of a tsp into 1 tbsp of vinegar. If it bubbles, it's fresh. Otherwise, time to get a new batch!

NUTS

Walnuts, almonds, pistachios, hazelnuts, peanuts. Most nuts are interchangeable, so if you prefer one over another, go right ahead! If you don't prefer nuts for medical or other reasons, they can always be substituted with dried fruit like raisins, cranberries, dried blueberries, etc. If nuts form a part of the flour mix in a recipe, you could substitute an equal amount with a flour, but expect a slight change in texture or taste, maybe both.

A word of caution: check dates and storage conditions while buying nuts. Improperly stored or old produce goes rancid easily, so best to buy a small batch first. If possible, do a taste test if the seller allows it. I store all nuts in the freezer during summer, and often use them directly out of there.

Nut Meal: Nut meals are now easily available online and in specialty stores. The other option is to make your own. If the recipe requires X grams of nut meal, I grind X grams of whole nuts with 1 or 2 tbsp of flour/sugar (depending on whether the recipe contains flour or not), reducing the same amount of flour/sugar from the ingredient list. Grind in a nut grinder with short, quick pulses to ensure that the nuts don't leave oil. If it's part of a dry mix, I normally just throw everything into the jar of a processor and give it all a good grind together. This ensures the nuts grind well, and as a bonus mix well too, so there's no need to sift the mix.

CHIA SEEDS

I always have a jar each of white and black chia seeds since I use them often while baking, in desserts and in my everyday morning smoothie. Both work well and can be used interchangeably. Often the easiest way to make a quick pudding, chia seeds are sometimes a handy substitute for eggs. 1 tbsp of chia seeds + 3 tbsp of water stirred together well and left to stand to gel for 4–5 minutes, then stirred again, is my standard recipe to replace an egg in some recipes.

FLAVOURS I LIKE USING IN DESSERT

Coffee: My most favourite pairing with chocolate; I think they were meant to be together. I use any available instant coffee powder, from Davidoff to Sunrise or Bru. They all work really well.

Garam Masala: Most often used in savoury stir fries and curries in the subcontinent, you'll be pleasantly surprised at how well garam masala pairs with chocolate. Think pumpkin pie spice, then think garam masala. This quintessential Indian spice mix lends beautiful flavour to puddings, fruit cake and truffles too. To start you off, perhaps try my popular Garam Masala Chocolate Pudding (page 175).

I have two simple basic garam masala recipes (page 267) in the 'Basics to Bottles' chapter, one for the standard Indian kitchen, the other an Indian version of pie spice. You could use either, else use a standard garam masala mix from your kitchen or your favourite brand.

Vanilla: From a scraped vanilla bean, to home-made vanilla extract to vanilla sugar, real vanilla is quite magical, elevating the ordinary to something quite special. You can find a vanilla extract and vanilla sugar recipe in the 'Basics to Bottles' chapter at the end of the book.

Orange: The zest of a fresh orange (keenu/maalta, as they are known locally) can do loads to lift a simple dessert. Rub the zest into sugar to give you instant orange sugar, or add it directly into puddings or cake for a burst of freshness. It pairs really well with chocolate and is a favourite when oranges are in season.

Tea: My love of using tea leaves in desserts came from using Anandini Himalaya Tea, which does beautiful blends. From flavouring clarified butter/ghee with tea leaves, to steeping coconut milk with them, I find the possibilities infinitely interesting.

Lime: A citrusy burst of fresh lime goes really well with white chocolate.

SETTING/THICKENING AGENTS

Setting of desserts might vary if you use a chocolate different from what is mentioned in the recipe.

Gelatine: My stock of gelatine is from overseas since I always stock up on it while travelling. Gelatine is a non-vegetarian product, and I find small differences across brands. Please use the one you like. It might take a little experimentation to get the right set.

Agar Agar: The vegetarian alternative to gelatine, I find the strength of agar agar a little more as compared to gelatine. I use one from Urban Platter. Please use the one you like. It might take a little experimentation to get the right set.

Cornflour: I use this often to thicken puddings.

EGGS

Free-range.

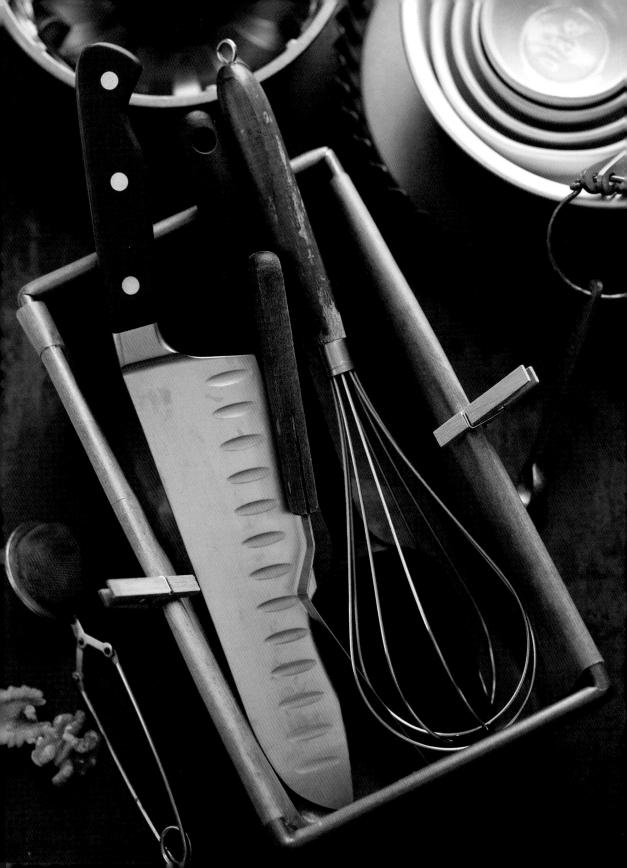

The Tools of My Trade

You don't have to have a kitchen with state-of-the-art appliances to churn out bakes or desserts. A basic oven, two bowls and a whisk are sometimes all I need, things that got me by quite well when I began baking and spending time in the kitchen.

I am still the same fuss-free baker (I call myself 'the lazy baker') and often throw caution to the wind. Most of my bakes are simple dry mixes and wet mixes which come together to form the batter. If the dry mix has a cocoa powder, I might sift it, since cocoa powder forms small lumps if stirred in directly. Along with two bowls and a whisk, here's a list of things that make life easier in my kitchen.

Oven: The conventional countertop oven is the heart of my kitchen and the one thing I turn on almost every morning. I use a 42L Borosil OTG that snugly fits in two round 8 inch cake tins at one time, while my other oven is the 60L Morphy Richards. Both work equally well, yet each behaves differently. It's worth experimenting to find your oven's sweet spot. Your model's user manual is a good guide.

Baking Tins/Trays: If the oven needs to be good, the tins and trays matter just as much. Good, reputed brands, heavy-duty trays and tins ensure even baking with uniform distribution of heat and can last a lifetime.

A good beginning might be a mix of the following, or perhaps all!

- 6 and 8 inch round, loose-bottomed tart tin
- 6, 7 and 8 inch round cake tin (loose-bottomed is always a good idea)
- 8 inch square baking tin (loose-bottomed is my favourite)
- 6 or 12 cavity muffin tray
- 9 x 5 inch loaf tin
- 2–3 cookie trays

A jelly roll pan, maybe a few dessert rings and an adjustable large dessert ring are also good to own. If you're in the mood to add more, a Bundt tin is a really good addition. You can keep adding to these basics once you know this is going to be fun and something you will do often! Amazon has almost everything you will need. Brands I like are Amazon Basics and Meyer.

Do make sure the trays and tins you order fit into the oven, or be ready to gift them to grateful friends. Been there, done that!

Weighing Scale: The cheapest and best baking investment I ever made. Amazon has digital weighing scales that cost a few hundred rupees, and if you are a keen baker, a weighing scale is a must-have. I have included a conversion chart at the end of this chapter to help in the interim.

Electric Hand-Mixer: A sturdy electric hand-blender takes care of most of your needs till you are ready to upgrade and invest in a stand mixer! I use Hamilton Beach currently and it works well.

Stand Mixer: It's always handy to have a stand mixer if you bake often, though definitely not mandatory. I survived my first eight years of baking without one. I now have one, and I have to say it's a luxury to own and makes life very simple. A one-bowl cookie dough like the Salted Butter and Chocolate Chunk Wholegrain Shortbread (page 106) comes together in minutes, as does home-made butter, to name a couple of things.

Blender/Grinder: Get a sturdy blender with a sturdy jar, a tight-fitting lid and a good set of blades. Most blenders these days come with a smaller spice/nut grinder. That's a really handy attachment and works well to make small batches of nut meal or oat flour.

Nut Grinder: If your blender doesn't come with the spice/nut grinder attachment, this is a must-have. Great to make a quick nut meal, see 'Nut Meal' in the 'My Pantry Essentials' section of this book.

Manual Chopper: From chopping soft nuts like walnuts and pistachio to a quick fruit coulis, I find this non-electrical magic gadget really handy. Amazon has a great selection.

Silicon Spatula: The best standard type of mixers and bowl cleaners, these are great to get the last bits of ingredients out of food processors. Two or three graded sizes are good to have.

Good Knives: Standard equipment in the kitchen, from Santoku knives to peelers and choppers, good brands will last you a lifetime. Victorinox is a favourite, as is Ergo Chef. Make sure you keep one heavy knife to chop chocolate, and a good-quality firm, serrated one to slice biscotti and fruit.

Strainer/Sifter: I have three or four different sizes on hand, from large ones to sift a dry mix to medium ones that are quite handy to strain a coulis. Small sifts are perfect for a quick dusting over of powdered sugar, cinnamon, cocoa powder, etc.

Whisks: I have these in several sizes and use them equally. Most handy to have in the kitchen, quite a few of my recipes in the book depend on this invention, where often a bowl and a whisk can create magic!

Glass Bowls: The more the merrier—let's just say you can never have enough! I have a cupboardful in every size possible. Really handy to do the 'mise en place' or prep, I measure and line up everything before I begin working on a recipe, which makes life so much easier!

Chopping Board: Handy for chopping everything from chocolate, to nuts, to fruit, to slicing biscotti. I like to keep separate chopping boards for desserts.

Measuring Spoons/Cups: Even though I weigh my ingredients to bake, smaller amounts like baking powder, baking soda, salt, coffee, cinnamon powder, garam masala and vanilla extract are almost always spoon measures. An equal volume of different ingredients might not have the same weight; hence, a weighing scale is a more precise option. For smaller quantities, however, measuring spoons work fine.

Offset Spatula: Great handy tool for frosting/icing, or to uniformly spread batter or filling.

Microplane Zester: It is a gem to have on hand for orange and lime zest, or even the quick nutmeg grate!

Cooling Rack: I have four or five for the amount of baking I do. However, one would be a good beginning.

Baking Parchment: Life does not get easier than this. For an easy clean-up with no unnecessary sticking, I always have a few rolls of parchment paper on hand. I wouldn't survive without them.

Miscellaneous: Aluminium foil, clingwrap, silicon mats, piping bags, nozzles, doilies, cupcake liners, wooden picks . . . the list goes on!

KITCHEN CONVERSION TABLE

Weight	Spoon/Cup Measure (1 cup = 237 ml)
65 g all-purpose flour	½ cup
130 g wholewheat flour	1 cup
30 g besan/gram flour	⅓ cup
100 g brown sugar	½ cup
75 g coconut sugar	½ cup
115 g castor sugar	½ cup
70 g jaggery powder	½ cup
100 g butter *or* 100 g clarified butter/ghee	½ cup
240 ml milk *or* 240 ml buttermilk	1 cup
50 g cocoa powder	½ cup
15 g cocoa powder	2 tbsp
40 g quick-cooking oats	½ cup
50 g walnuts	½ cup
65 g almonds	½ cup

Making the Most of My Book

Living in India and working with chocolate is quite an experience. How chocolate behaves in summer versus how well it behaves in winter is quite an eye-opener, as is the revelation that couverture and compound chocolate are so different at every level. At the cost of repeating myself, I only use couverture chocolate.

My experience has taught me that chocolate can be quite temperamental to work with, yet it is easy to tame. If you follow a few simple rules, you should be fine. Basically, chocolate doesn't like sudden changes in temperature. Gradual is good, and patience is a virtue. Be gentle, give it time and you will love working with chocolate like I do.

HANDLING CHOCOLATE

The microwave is handy while melting chocolate, but slow and steady wins here: 20 to 30 second bursts of power, stir, repeat as required. I, however, go with the double-boiler method since it gives me better control. Place the finely chopped chocolate in a squeaky clean glass bowl. Bring some water to a simmering boil in a saucepan. Place the glass bowl on top of the saucepan, making sure the bottom of the bowl doesn't touch the water. Stir now and then while the chocolate melts gradually. It's imperative to make sure the bowl in which the chocolate is being melted is completely dry. Even a trace of moisture will cause the chocolate to seize.

For storing chocolate, a cool, dark and dry place works best. However, given the weather conditions in India during summer and monsoon, I store my chocolate in the fridge. Not ideal, but it works.

While working with truffles, keep the touch minimal and quick. Chocolate tends to melt with exposure to body heat through the palms and sticks to them.

When all else fails, there is always ganache! Getting a whipping cream frosting has been an uphill task for me. Whether it is the ambient temperature or the kind of whipping cream available here, I find it difficult to whip up the cream to a suitable consistency. A quick ganache to frost the simplest of cakes always works in making them more attractive (you can find the recipe in the 'Basics to Bottles', chapter, page 248). A white chocolate ganache is a little more complex. I use a 2:1 chocolate to cream ratio, and overnight refrigeration to firm it up. I often whip it before use.

SOME CRUMBS TO PONDER...

- Quality ingredients are **key**.
- Read once, read twice to make sure you have all the ingredients.
- Line up the ingredients before you begin making the dessert. A 'mise en place' or pre-preparation of having all the ingredients lined up makes life easy.
- If pushed for time, try and break up the process into steps, especially when attempting recipes from the 'Special-Occasion Cakes' section.
- I use wholegrains and non-refined sugars where possible. You can use all-purpose flour and everyday sugar if you like. Expect a small difference in the baking time, taste and texture.
- While baking, use ingredients at room temperature, unless mentioned otherwise.
- Get a weighing scale. Once you get used to a weighing scale, life becomes simpler, and recipes get more predictable.
- Use the right tin size as specified in the recipe. A different size will probably give a different outcome.
- Know your oven, set a timer, make it a habit to check five minutes before the suggested time since every oven behaves differently, as do baking tins/trays.
- From experience, I find that the setting time and sometimes the outcome of recipes differs with seasons, especially temperature, elevation and humidity. Being intuitive helps.
- Familiarize yourself with simple techniques like melting chocolate, folding batter, checking for doneness, quick garnishes.
- Be patient. It is sometimes important to wait for a bake to cool completely, or for a cold dessert to set. For instance, eggless bakes usually need a longer cooling time to be able to cut neat slices.

Do tag me on Instagram **@passionateaboutbaking** if you make or experiment with the recipes. I would love to hear from you!

Teacakes

These are one of my most made sorts of cakes that date back to a phase where I was charmed by simple, fuss-free pound cakes, with standard recipes that had expected outcomes and were easy for young hands (my kids) to slice. Pound cakes, simple Bundt cakes, chocolate-chip coffee cakes and 'malai'/ top-of-the-milk cakes were all part of this phase. I revisited this phase during the pandemic, where simple and fuss-free recipes saw new light. These trying times proved once again that chocolate can comfort you and make you happy.

Double Chocolate & Banana
WHOLEGRAIN BUNDT

🍴 MAKES 1 LARGE BUNDT

A deeply delicious and moist teacake that baked like magic in this beautiful Bundt tin from Nordicware. This is a popular old recipe that has been tested by many. It's a dense, deeply chocolatey teacake this is 100% wholegrain. I kept adding ingredients, beginning with ripe bananas, into the bowl of my stand mixer, and it churned out a great batter. It's as easily made with a bowl, fork and whisk.

INGREDIENTS

225 g bananas or **3** large, ripe bananas, mashed
150 g coconut sugar
2 eggs
100 g clarified butter/ghee, melted
130 g wholewheat flour
50 g cocoa powder
1 tsp baking soda
A pinch of salt
1 tsp vanilla extract
75 g dark chocolate chips

METHOD

Preheat the oven to 180°C. Grease well and dust a twelve-cup Bundt tin with cocoa powder. Make sure you leave no spots uncovered.
In the bowl of a stand mixer, whisk the bananas and coconut sugar at medium speed until smooth.
Alternatively, use a large bowl and an electric hand-mixer or a whisk.
Add the eggs, clarified butter/ghee, flour, cocoa powder, baking soda, salt and vanilla extract and mix together at low speed.
Add the chocolate chips last, and mix briefly to incorporate.
Turn into the prepared Bundt tin. Tap on the counter to level the batter.
Bake at 180°C for approximately 45 minutes to an hour, or until a toothpick tester comes out clean. Tent the top with a sheet of aluminium foil in the last 10–15 minutes if the top is over-browning.
Cool in the tin for at least 30 minutes, then demould and cool on the rack.
Serve sliced, warm or at room temperature.

Optional: Top it with a chocolate ganache or salted caramel drizzle.

WHAT IF?

If you don't have coconut sugar, you can use brown sugar instead.
If you don't have a Bundt tin, this can be made in a 9 x 5 inch loaf tin.

Dark Chocolate & Walnut
WHOLEWHEAT CAKE

MAKES ONE 9 x 5 INCH LOAF

A nostalgic favourite, this cake brings back memories of the quintessential 'malai' cakes from yesteryear. Back then, many Indian households used to boil milk, collect the layer of cream or malai appearing on top of the milk, use some as is, then make sweet butter from the rest. The more adventurous ones would bake a delicious, homey comforting cake with malai. This is my rendition of those good old days!

INGREDIENTS

DRY MIX

175 g wholewheat flour
1 tsp baking powder
½ tsp baking soda
A pinch of salt

WET MIX

130 g milk cream/malai
175 g jaggery powder
2 eggs
50 g cocoa powder
½ tsp vanilla bean paste
(or 1 tsp vanilla extract)
150 ml buttermilk
75 g dark chocolate chips
75 g walnuts, chopped

TOPPING
Walnut halves, chocolate chips

METHOD

Preheat the oven to 170°C. Line a 9 x 5 inch loaf tin with parchment paper.

Whisk together the dry ingredients in a small bowl. Reserve.

In the bowl of a stand mixer, beat the milk cream/malai and jaggery powder until light. Beat in the eggs one by one, followed by the cocoa powder and vanilla bean paste.

Alternatively, use a large bowl and an electric hand-mixer.

Add one-third of the reserved dry mix to the wet mix. Fold in with a spatula, then add in one-third of the buttermilk. Fold in. Repeat twice.

Gently fold in the chocolate chips and walnuts.

Turn into the prepared tin and spread uniformly. Sprinkle the top with walnut halves and chocolate chips. Tap sharply on the counter once to level the batter.

Bake for approximately an hour, until a toothpick tester comes out clean. Check at 45 minutes, and tent the top with a sheet of foil if it begins browning too soon.

Cool in the tin for about 20 minutes, then gently take out of the tin and cool on the cooling rack.

Slice warm or at room temperature.

Everyday Quick Chocolate
BUTTERMILK POUND CAKE

⚒ MAKES ONE 9 x 5 INCH LOAF

This is a twist on a popular lime buttermilk pound cake recipe on my blog, one I have baked in several avatars. Here is the chocolate version. Perfect comfort food with that cup of tea or coffee, or with milk for the kids, this is a pretty accommodative recipe and responds well to change! It's also a good cake to take to a picnic.

INGREDIENTS

DRY MIX

175 g wholewheat flour
35 g cocoa powder
1 tsp baking powder
½ tsp baking soda
A pinch of salt

WET MIX

100 g clarified butter/ghee, room temperature
200 g brown sugar
2 eggs
1 tsp vanilla extract
1 tbsp instant coffee powder
80 g thick yogurt
50 ml buttermilk
100 g dark chocolate chips

TOPPING

50 g dark chocolate chips

METHOD

Preheat the oven to 170°C. Line the sides and bottom of a 9 x 5 inch loaf tin.

Sift together the dry ingredients. Reserve in a bowl.

In the bowl of a stand mixer, whisk together the clarified butter/ghee and sugar on high speed until light and fluffy. Beat in the eggs one by one, followed by the vanilla extract, then the coffee powder, and last, the yogurt. Alternatively, use a large bowl and an electric hand-mixer. On the lowest speed, fold in half the dry mix, then half the buttermilk. Repeat with the remaining dry mix, then the remaining buttermilk. Fold in the chocolate chips.

Turn the batter into the prepared tin, and sprinkle over chocolate chips.

Bake for approximately 45–50 minutes until a toothpick tester comes out clean.

Cool in the tin for about 30 minutes, then gently take the cake out of the tin and cool on the cooling rack.

Dark Chocolate & Fresh Plum
WHOLEWHEAT GATEAU

MAKES ONE 7 INCH GATEAU

This 100% wholewheat fallen gateau is one I bake in late summer every year when plums are at their sweetest! It is indulgent, deeply fudgy and earthy, with mild undertones of fresh plums. The ganache frosting on top completes the luxury. I've tried to break down the steps to ease the process. The three wet mixes might appear complicated, but once you read through, they 'flow'!

INGREDIENTS

DRY MIX

75 g wholewheat flour
¾ tsp baking soda
A pinch of salt

WET MIX 1

100 g dark chocolate, chopped fine
185 g fresh plum purée (of about 4 medium pitted plums, with skin)
2 egg yolks
40 g cocoa powder
½ vanilla bean scraped (or **1 tsp** vanilla extract)

WET MIX 2

2 egg whites
⅛ tsp cream of tartar
100 g brown sugar

WET MIX 3

100 g unsalted butter, softened
85 g brown sugar

METHOD

Preheat the oven to 180ºC. Line a 7 inch loose-bottomed tin with parchment paper.

Whisk together the dry ingredients in a small bowl. Reserve.

Place the chocolate in a heatproof bowl. Microwave for 30 seconds at a time until the chocolate melts, or melt using the double-boiler method.
Using a small balloon whisk, whisk the melted chocolate until smooth, then whisk in the plum purée, followed by the egg yolks, one at a time. Lastly, whisk in the cocoa powder and scraped vanilla bean, making sure the mixture is smooth. Reserve.

In the bowl of a stand mixer, beat the egg whites and cream of tartar to soft peaks. Add 100 g sugar, 1 tbsp at a time, and continue to beat to stiff peaks. Reserve in a glass bowl.
Alternatively, use a large bowl and an electric hand-mixer.

Add the butter and sugar to the bowl of the stand mixer (the same one used to beat the egg whites in), and beat for a couple of minutes until light and fluffy.
Fold in the dry mix, followed by wet mix 1, and stir until smooth. Lastly, gently fold in wet mix 2.

Transfer the batter into the prepared tin.

Bake for approximately an hour or until a toothpick tester comes out with a few moist crumbs. Tent the top with a sheet of aluminium foil if the top is over-browning. Top as follows.

Place on the cooling rack and leave to cool in the tin for about 30 minutes.

Gently turn out of the tin, and cool completely on the cooling rack. Top with ganache.

Garnish with seasonal fruit and fresh mint.

CHOCOLATE GANACHE

75 g bittersweet chocolate, chopped fine
100 ml cream

TOPPING
Stone fruit in season, fresh mint

Place the chocolate in a glass bowl.

Heat the cream till hot but not boiling and pour over the chocolate.

Allow to stand for 10–15 minutes until the chocolate softens, then stir gently until smooth.

*(**Note:** Serve with seasonal fruit like a cherry/plum compote and single cream for an elegant dessert.)*

WHAT IF?

If you don't have plums, you can use blueberries instead.

Spicy Chocolate Garam Masala
FRUIT CAKE

🍴 **MAKES ONE 6 INCH CAKE**

One bite of this cake will transport you to a winter wonderland where warm spices, chocolate and rum embrace you with their warmth. The flavours come together really well, and each crumb screams holiday season!

My holiday baking through winter has increasingly been flavoured by garam masala, a spice my mother used to lace her Christmas fruit cake with. It comes as a surprise to many since they associate this quintessential Indian spice with curries, kebabs and savoury food.

INGREDIENTS

FRUIT MIX

150 g dried fruit (raisins, dried berries, apricots, orange peel, crystallized ginger, etc.)
150 ml rum
2 tbsp garam masala (page 267)
2 tbsp coconut sugar

DRY MIX

65 g all-purpose flour
40 g almond meal
20 g cocoa powder
1 tsp baking powder
½ tsp baking soda
A pinch of salt
100 g walnuts, chopped
85 g dark chocolate chips

WET MIX

75 g clarified butter/ghee, melted
150 g coconut sugar
1 egg
1 tbsp Greek yogurt
1 tsp vanilla extract
30 ml rum (to soak)

METHOD

Stir the ingredients for the fruit mix and store in a covered glass jar/bowl for a minimum of 2–3 days. Check daily and top the mix with more rum if required.
Preheat the oven to 160°C. Line a 6 inch loose-bottomed tin with parchment paper.

Stir together the dry ingredients in a bowl to mix.
Toss the fruit mix into the dry mix, using a fork to coat the fruit with the flour. Reserve.

In the bowl of a stand mixer, beat the clarified butter/ghee and coconut sugar until light and mousse-like.
Alternatively, use a large bowl and an electric hand-mixer.
Beat in the egg, followed by the Greek yogurt and vanilla extract.
Fold the dry mix into the wet mix.
Transfer to the prepared tin, even out and bake for approximately an hour until done.

RUM-SPIKED CHOCOLATE GANACHE

75 g dark chocolate, chopped fine
100 ml cream
½ tsp garam masala
1 tbsp rum

Place the chocolate in a glass bowl. Heat the cream till hot but not boiling and pour over the chocolate. Allow to stand for 10–15 minutes until the chocolate softens, add the garam masala and rum, then stir gently until smooth. Cool to a spreadable consistency.

TOPPING

Candied orange slices, berries, cocoa powder

Top the cooled cake with the ganache, then garnish with candied orange slices, berries etc.
Dust the edges with cocoa powder.

Banana Walnut Chocolate Chip
LOAF

MAKES ONE 9 x 5 INCH LOAF

I was never a fan of bananas in baking, yet I baked this on popular request. This teacake turned out 'unbelievably good', as the better half declared. It's really good for a wholegrain banana bread, where ghee meets coconut sugar to create beautiful caramel undertones. Do make sure the bananas are overripe.

The loaf's packed with toasted walnuts and dark chocolate chips and vanishes pretty quickly, and soon I'm waiting for bananas to get overripe again! Another fuss-free, one-bowl recipe that's hand-mixed, and simple enough even for kids to stir together, it's great for breakfast, tea or gifting, for anytime actually.

INGREDIENTS

DRY MIX

130 g wholewheat flour
65 g all-purpose flour
1 tsp baking soda
1 tsp cinnamon powder
½ tsp salt
50 g walnuts, chopped
50 g dark chocolate chips

WET MIX

100 g clarified butter/ghee
melted, cooled
100 g sugar
100 g coconut sugar
2 large eggs (or 2 small eggs +
1 yolk)
1 tsp vanilla extract
150 g bananas or **2** large,
ripe bananas, mashed
1 tbsp Greek yogurt

TOPPING

Walnut halves, chocolate chips

METHOD

Preheat the oven to 180ºC. Line a 9 x 5 inch loaf tin with parchment paper.

Stir together the dry ingredients in a bowl to mix. Reserve.

In a large bowl, whisk together the clarified butter/ghee and both sugars.

Whisk in the eggs one by one, followed by the vanilla extract, Greek yogurt and mashed bananas.

Add the dry mix into the wet mix, mixing until just combined. Do not over-mix.

Transfer the batter to the prepared tin, and top with walnut halves and chocolate chips.

Bake at 180ºC for approximately an hour, or until a toothpick tester comes out clean.

Cool in the tin for at least 30 minutes, then gently take it out and cool on the cooling rack.

Serve warm or at room temperature.

Banana Walnut Chocolate Chip
LOAF (EGGLESS)

🍴 MAKES ONE 9 x 5 INCH LOAF

When I shared the Banana Walnut Chocolate Chip Loaf video on my Instagram account, loads of people ended up making it because it was so simple. I also received a ton of messages requesting an eggless version. I tried making it a couple of times but wasn't happy with the outcome. Then, one morning, three overripe bananas stared me in the face, and I gave the recipe another shot. Ever so simply, an eggless version fell into place. Just skipping the eggs and Greek yogurt and adding an extra banana turned out a perfect eggless banana loaf! I was quite chuffed with this one!

INGREDIENTS

DRY MIX

130 g wholewheat flour
60 g all-purpose flour
1 tsp baking soda
1 tsp baking powder
A pinch of salt
50 g walnuts, chopped
80 g dark chocolate chips

WET MIX

100 g clarified butter/ghee, melted
50 g sugar
75 g coconut sugar
225 g bananas or **3 large**, ripe bananas, mashed
1 tsp vanilla extract

TOPPING

Walnut halves, chocolate chips

METHOD

Preheat the oven to 180ºC. Line a 9 x 5 inch loaf tin with parchment paper.

Stir together the dry ingredients in a bowl to mix. Reserve.

In a large bowl, whisk together the clarified butter/ghee and both sugars, followed by the mashed bananas and vanilla extract.
Add the dry mix and fold in until just combined. Do not over-mix.
Transfer the batter into the prepared tin, and top with walnut halves and chocolate chips.
Bake for approximately 40 minutes, or until a toothpick tester comes out clean. Tent the top with a sheet of aluminium foil in the last 10–15 minutes if the top is over-browning.
Cool in the tin for 30 minutes at least, then turn it out gently and cool on the cooling rack.
Serve warm or at room temperature.

Dark Chocolate

SHEET CAKE (EGGLESS)

🍴 MAKES ONE 8 INCH SQUARE CAKE

This sheet cake really surprised us! Surprised us that something so simple could taste so good. A one-bowl cake with a whipped ganache frosting, this is one of those recipes you can throw together in minutes. Ghee, strongly brewed coffee and buttermilk make the cake deep, dark, chocolatey and very moist. The recipe works for a layered cake as well as cupcakes.

INGREDIENTS

DRY MIX

120 g all-purpose flour
½ tsp baking soda
½ tsp baking powder
¼ tsp salt

WET MIX

1 egg or **1** chia egg (1 tbsp chia seeds + 3 tbsp water)
50 g clarified butter/ghee, melted, cooled
200 g brown sugar
1 tsp vanilla extract
50 g cocoa powder
115 ml buttermilk
90 ml strongly brewed coffee, warm (or 3 tsp instant coffee powder + hot water)

WHIPPED CHOCOLATE GANACHE

100 g bittersweet chocolate, chopped fine
150 ml cream
1 tbsp clarified butter/ghee

TOPPING

Berries, cocoa nibs

METHOD

Preheat the oven to 180°C. Line an 8 x 8 inch square loose-bottomed baking tin with parchment paper.

Whisk together the dry ingredients in a small bowl. Reserve.

In a small bowl, stir together the water and chia seeds. Leave to stand for 5 minutes to gel while you mix the other ingredients.
In the bowl of a stand mixer, whisk together the clarified butter/ghee, sugar and vanilla on high speed until light and fluffy.
Alternatively, use a large bowl and an electric hand-mixer.
Add the chia egg and whisk again, followed by the cocoa powder and buttermilk. The mixture might look a little curdled, but don't worry.
On the lowest speed, add in half the dry mix, then half the brewed coffee, followed by the remaining dry mix, then the rest of the brewed coffee.
Transfer to the prepared tin and bake for about 35 minutes, until a toothpick tester comes out clean.
Cool the cake in the tin for 15–20 minutes, then gently lift it out. Frost the cake with the whipped ganache, and top with dried berries, cocoa nibs, etc. Cool completely on the rack.

Place the chocolate in a glass bowl.
Heat the cream till hot but not boiling and pour over the chocolate.
Allow to stand for 10–15 minutes until the chocolate softens, then add the clarified butter/ghee and stir gently until smooth. Repeat twice after every 20 minutes.
Allow to rest for 30 minutes in the fridge, then beat on high speed with a hand-blender until light and mousse-like.

Nutella & Raspberry
MADELEINES (EGGLESS)

🍴 MAKES 16

I've long been fascinated by madeleines, these delicate little shell-shaped butter cakes that are originally from France. This recipe is based on the Eggless Almond Lime Raspberry Ghee Madeleines shared on my blog, and a jar of Nutella that needed a destination. I played around with ingredients and was rewarded with these little beauties.

Dipping them into melted white couverture chocolate took them to a happy new level, and freeze-dried raspberries added that pop of colour and a slight tang.

INGREDIENTS

DRY MIX

30 g wholewheat flour
100 g all-purpose flour
1 tsp baking powder
A pinch of salt
2 tbsp crushed, freeze-dried raspberries (optional)

WET MIX

40 g cocoa powder
120 ml milk, room temperature
70 g clarified butter/ghee, melted, tepid
50 g Nutella
50 g brown sugar
½ tsp vanilla bean paste or vanilla extract

TOPPING

100 g white couverture chocolate, melted, cooled

METHOD

Preheat the oven to 180°C. Sparingly grease a 12-mould madeleine pan with clarified butter/ghee.

Whisk together the dry ingredients in a small bowl. Reserve.

In another bowl, whisk the cocoa powder into the milk, then whisk in the ghee, Nutella, brown sugar and vanilla bean paste.
Stir the dry mix into the wet mix, then ladle into the madeleine mould cavities. Tap gently.
Bake for approximately 14–15 minutes until a toothpick tester comes out clean.
Turn the madeleines gently on to a cooling rack, and leave to cool completely.
Dip the tops into the melted white chocolate, and sprinkle over crushed, freeze-dried raspberries. Leave to set. If it's very warm, set for 10 minutes in the fridge.

WHAT IF?

If you don't have a madeleine tray, you can bake these in a mini muffin tray.

Coffee Chocolate Chip
WHOLEWHEAT CAKE (EGGLESS)

MAKES ONE 4 INCH CAKE

Most of us have one cake that we bake most often, and for years, mine was a Wholegrain Coffee Chocolate Chip Pound Cake. Recently, I decided to create an eggless version. Oh my, it turned out so good.

This is a small 4 inch cake, the ingredients all simple with easy substitutes. Like most of my quick recipes, it's a basic dry mix + wet mix, two-bowl, hand-mixed one. I baked it in this pretty, fluted, kugelhopf tin that I've had for years. Fluted tins always have a childlike charm, an oooh! factor if the cake leaves the sides clean. This one did!

INGREDIENTS

DRY MIX

130 g wholewheat flour
½ tsp baking powder
½ tsp baking soda
A pinch of salt
50 g dark chocolate chips

WET MIX

100 g brown sugar
55 g clarified butter/ghee
1 chia egg (1 tbsp chia seeds + 3 tbsp water)
2 tbsp strong coffee (1 tbsp instant coffee powder + 1 tbsp boiling water)
75 ml buttermilk
25 g thick yogurt
1 tsp vanilla extract

CHOCOLATE GANACHE

75 g dark chocolate, chopped fine
100 ml cream
1 tsp instant coffee powder
1 tbsp honey

METHOD

Preheat the oven to 180°C. Grease a 4 inch kugelhopf tin/mini Bundt/jelly-baking mould or round tin with ghee and dust with flour.

Stir together the dry ingredients in a bowl to mix. Reserve.

In a small bowl, stir together the water and chia seeds. Leave to stand for 5 minutes to gel while you mix the other ingredients.
Place the sugar in a large bowl. Heat the clarified butter/ghee and pour over the sugar. Whisk well, then whisk in the strong coffee, chia egg, buttermilk, yogurt and vanilla extract.
Now stir in the dry mix. Don't over-mix.
Transfer the batter to the prepared tin. Tap the tin gently on the counter to even out the batter.
Bake for approximately 30 minutes until done and a toothpick tester comes out clean. Leave in the tin for about 20 minutes before gently loosening the edges with a butter knife and turning out to cool completely on the cooling rack.
Top with a dark chocolate ganache or serve as is.

Place the chocolate in a glass bowl.
Heat the cream till hot but not boiling and pour over the chocolate.
Allow to stand for 10–15 minutes until the chocolate softens, Add the coffee and honey, then stir gently until smooth. Repeat twice after every 20 minutes. Cool to a spreadable consistency.

Four-Minute Microwave
QUARANTINE CHOCOLATE CAKE
(EGGLESS)

▯▯ MAKES ONE 4 INCH CAKE

Once I discovered that I could 'bake' cookies in the microwave, my joy knew no bounds. It was like a brand-new world had opened up. This was fairly recent, following the cookies my daughter made (Two-Minute Microwave Wholegrain Chocolate Chip Cookies [Eggless], page 114) during the pandemic-induced lockdown.

This cake has a connect to things I really enjoy: baking, chocolate, going egg-free, using wholegrains, simple bakes and basic ingredients.

INGREDIENTS

DRY MIX

100 g wholewheat flour
½ tsp baking powder
¼ tsp baking soda
50 g walnuts, chopped
25 g dark chocolate chips
A pinch of salt

WET MIX

70 g jaggery powder
50 g clarified butter/ghee, melted
25 g cocoa powder
75 g bananas or **1** large, ripe banana, mashed
75 g thick yogurt
1 tsp vanilla extract

TOPPING
Walnut halves, chocolate chips

METHOD

Line the bottom and sides of a 4 inch microwave-safe glass baking dish.

Stir together the dry ingredients in a bowl to mix. Reserve.

Place the jaggery powder in a bowl. Heat the clarified butter/ghee till hot and pour over the jaggery powder. Whisk well, then whisk in the cocoa powder, mashed banana, yogurt and vanilla extract.
Add the dry mix to the wet mix and stir gently to combine. Don't over-mix.
Transfer the batter to the prepared dish. Top with walnut halves and chocolate chips.
Bake at full microwave oven power for 3½ minutes. Open and check with a toothpick tester. It should come out clean with a few moist crumbs, else bake for another 30 seconds.
Cool for 30 minutes in the baking dish, then gently turn out to cool on the cooling rack.

WHAT IF?

If you don't have jaggery powder, you can use brown sugar instead.

Chocolate Walnut Olive Oil
CAKE (EGGLESS)

MAKES ONE 6 INCH CAKE

This was one of the first eggless cakes I ever baked, and both butter and olive oil work equally well for it. The walnuts scattered on top get nicely toasted and add a great texture. The key thing is to let the cake cool and chill for a couple of hours to get neat slices. If you don't mind a crumbly cake because waiting is not your strength, dive right in. Either way, this cake pleases!

INGREDIENTS

DRY MIX

65 g all-purpose flour
65 g wholewheat flour
50 g cocoa powder
1 tbsp coffee powder
A pinch of salt
25 g walnuts, chopped
25 g dark chocolate chips

WET MIX

110 g coconut sugar
225 g full-fat yogurt (home-made)
1¼ tsp baking powder
½ tsp baking soda
100 ml light olive oil

TOPPINGS

Walnut halves, chocolate chips, vanilla/brown sugar

METHOD

Preheat the oven to 200°C. Line a round 6 inch tin with parchment paper.

Sift both the flours, cocoa powder, coffee powder and salt 2–3 times, then stir in the walnuts and chocolate chips. Reserve.

Beat the sugar and yogurt for 5 minutes at high speed. Add baking powder and baking soda, beat them in at low speed. Leave to stand for 3 minutes until bubbles appear as a reaction of the yogurt to the baking soda. Whisk in the olive oil.

Gently stir in the dry mix, a quarter at a time, blending in well after each addition.

Transfer the batter to the prepared tin. Tap the tin gently on the counter to even out the batter.

Sprinkle the top with walnut halves and chocolate chips, followed by a sprinkling of vanilla/brown sugar.

Bake at 200°C for 10 minutes, then reduce the temperature to 175°C and bake for 35–40 minutes or till a toothpick tester comes out clean.

Cool the cake in the tin for 20–30 minutes, then turn out and cool completely on the cooling rack.

Once cool, it is best refrigerated for 2–3 hours to get neat slices.

Nut & Berry Chocolate

BISCUIT CAKE (EGGLESS)

⚎ MAKES ONE 9 x 5 INCH CAKE

Said to be a favourite of Queen Elizabeth II and Prince William, the Nut & Berry Chocolate Biscuit Cake made by the Royal Kitchens of Buckingham Palace is an evergreen classic. Call it the quintessential biscuit cake, this no-bake refrigerator cake is indulgent and one that always pleases. Hardly any work, these are just a bunch of ingredients swathed in good-quality chocolate, then left to set in a shaped tin. This recipe is inspired by my friend Ruchira.

INGREDIENTS

140 g Cadbury Silk Hazelnut
150 g bittersweet chocolate, chopped fine
70 g unsalted butter, softened
30 g honey
125 g Marie biscuits/digestive biscuits, broken
100 g walnuts, chopped
70 g dried cranberries
50 g pistachio, chopped

TOPPING (OPTIONAL)

100 g dark chocolate , chopped fine
1 tbsp extra virgin olive oil

METHOD

Line a 9 x 5 inch tin with clingwrap hanging over the sides.

Place both the chocolates and butter in a large bowl and melt either in the microwave, 30 seconds at a time, or using the double-boiler method. Whisk until smooth.
Add in all the other ingredients and mix to make sure everything is coated well with the melted chocolate.
Transfer the mixture into the prepared tin, pressing down to push it into place. Level it out and chill for 4–6 hours.
Slice and serve.

In a small bowl, melt the chocolate and olive oil over either in a double boiler or in the microwave.
Pour this melted chocolate over the chilled biscuit cake and gently spread over uniformly. The chocolate will set quite soon, so garnish with rose petals, pistachio slivers and non-pareils immediately on pouring the melted chocolate.

WHAT IF?

If you don't have Cadbury, you can use any milk chocolate instead.

Tarts

I think tarts are most underrated as desserts. My feedback tells me that people sometimes find them intimidating. Rest assured, once you begin making them, you will find the charm addictive. Get the base sorted, figure out a few tricks and you'll be churning these out without batting an eyelid. Invest in a good-quality tart tin and there will be no looking back.

All the tart recipes under this section are eggless.

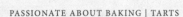

White Chocolate & Lime

WALNUT TART (GLUTEN-FREE)

🍴 MAKES ONE 6 INCH TART

This tart is as simple to make as it is delicious, and quite soothing too. I love white chocolate in desserts but use it sparingly as I keep only small batches in stock. Set in a dessert ring, the tart is a nice option for high tea or even a special occasion where it might work instead of a cake.

With just six ingredients, this recipe is also gluten-free. The base is light with a slightly crumbly texture that pairs beautifully with the luscious white chocolate filling.

You could make this vegan with a few substitutions, and flavour it as you like. Steeped tea, saffron, coffee, almond are all flavours that work well here. Treat the top as an empty canvas. That's one of my favourite ways to give desserts a signature touch!

INGREDIENTS

WALNUT BASE

175 g walnuts
40 g brown sugar
40 g clarified butter/ghee, melted, cooled

LIME & WHITE CHOCOLATE FILLING

200 ml cream
300 g white chocolate, chopped fine
15 g clarified butter/ghee, melted, cooled
Zest of **1** lime

TOPPING

Edible flowers, fruits, etc.

METHOD

Preheat the oven to 180°C. Line the outside of a 6 inch dessert ring with aluminium foil to make a base.

Place the walnuts and sugar in a dry grinder and process briefly until you get a breadcrumb-like mix. Make sure you don't over-process.
Stir in the clarified butter/ghee.
Transfer the mix to the base of the prepared ring, pressing gently but firmly into place.
Bake for 15 minutes until light golden and firm to the touch.
Leave to cool completely in the dessert ring, leaving the foil intact.

Place the chocolate in a glass bowl.
Heat the cream till hot but not boiling and pour over the chocolate.
Allow to stand for 10–15 minutes until the chocolate softens, then stir gently until smooth.
Stir in the clarified butter/ghee and the zest of 1 lime.
Pour the filling over the cooled walnut base.
Refrigerate for 4–6 hours or overnight to allow it to set.
Gently demould, and garnish as desired.

*(**Note:** The walnut base is slightly crumbly, so slice gently.)*

Chocolate & Salted Caramel
ALMOND OAT-CRUSTED TART

⚔ MAKES ONE 8 INCH TART

This tart has an interesting beginning. I had plenty of leftover crumb mix from a video I was shooting for Anzac-inspired bars (Almond Oat Salted Caramel Bars [Eggless], page 88). Since I absolutely loathe wasting anything, instead of reaching out for digestive biscuits for the tart base, I experimented with this mix. Best decision ever—this is a dessert that turned out as delicious as it was effortless. I knew I had to include this recipe in my book.

INGREDIENTS

TART BASE

50 g brown sugar
100 g all-purpose flour
100 g whole almonds
40 g quick-cooking oats
1 tsp baking soda
A pinch of salt
70 g clarified butter/ghee, melted, cooled

FILLING
250 g salted caramel sauce (page 255)
250 g dark chocolate, chopped fine
275 ml cream

METHOD

Preheat the oven to 180°C. Lightly grease an 8 inch loose-bottomed round tin or line an 8 inch dessert ring with heavy-duty aluminium foil.

Place the sugar, flour, almonds, oats, baking soda and salt in a food processor and process until you get a fine meal consistency. Alternatively, a dry grinder will work. Grind the almonds and flour together, making sure you do it in short pulses. Then whisk in the sugar and baking soda.

Add the clarified butter/ghee and process for a few seconds until mixed in.

Turn into the prepared tin and press into the base and work up the sides. Leave the sides uneven if you like.

Bake for 25 minutes until firm to the touch and light golden brown. While the shell is baking, prepare the filling.

Place the chocolate in a glass bowl.
Heat the cream till hot but not boiling and pour over the chocolate. Allow to stand for 10–15 minutes until the chocolate softens. Stir gently until smooth.

ASSEMBLE

Cool the baked tart base in the tin on the cooling rack for 10 minutes. Heat the salted caramel sauce and pour over the base of the shell. It should be quite runny. Swirl the tart tin around gently to coat the inner sides of the tart base.

TOPPING

Chocolate shards, cocoa powder, sea salt

Sit the tin back on the rack and gently pour in the warm chocolate filling. It should spread easily to fill the tart about halfway up.

Cool for about an hour, then refrigerate for 4–6 hours, or better still, overnight, to firm it up.

Top with frozen berries, fresh seasonal fruit or chocolate shards, etc., maybe a dusting of cocoa powder. Add in a sprig of fresh mint for that pop of colour.

(**Note:** *Can be made a day or two ahead. Keeps well for 2–3 days . . . if it lasts, that is!*)

WHAT IF?

If you don't want to use caramel, you can infuse the ganache with flavour, such as coffee, espresso, garam masala, liqueur, etc.

Chocolate & Salted Caramel
BUCKWHEAT TART (GLUTEN-FREE)

🍴 MAKES ONE 8 INCH TART

A simple, fuss-free, special-occasion recipe using buckwheat flour or kuttu ka atta as the base. It makes the tart gluten-free and no less delicious than any other. It looks quite stunning too. Salted caramel adds an indulgent layer over the delicate cookie base, which is then topped with a smooth and luxurious chocolate filling. I always have a jar of home-made salted caramel on hand.

You'll find a recipe for the salted caramel sauce in the 'Basics to Bottles' chapter (page 255).

INGREDIENTS

TART BASE

60 g buckwheat flour
85 g whole almonds
30 g cocoa powder
2 tbsp cornflour
2 tbsp brown sugar
A pinch of sea salt
75 g clarified butter/ghee, melted, cooled

CHOCOLATE FILLING

250 g salted caramel sauce (page 255)
250 g bittersweet chocolate, chopped fine
200 ml cream
75 g honey
30 g clarified butter/ghee

METHOD

Preheat the oven to 180°C. Lightly grease an 8 inch loose-bottomed tart tin.

Place all the ingredients except the clarified butter/ghee in a dry grinder and process until ground.

Whisk in the clarified butter/ghee, then gently mix with the fingertips until the mixture begins to come together and holds when pinched between the fingertips. Don't overwork the crumb.

Turn into the prepared tin. Press up the sides, then press the remaining crumb firmly to make the base.

Bake for approximately 15–20 minutes, until the edges are firm to the touch.

Pour salted caramel sauce over the base as the tart base comes out of the oven.

Leave to cool in the tart tin for 15–20 minutes, then add the filling.

Place the chocolate in a glass bowl.

Heat the cream till hot but not boiling and pour over the chocolate.

Allow to stand for 10–15 minutes until the chocolate softens, then add the honey and clarified butter/ghee and stir gently until smooth. Don't overwork it.

Pour this over the salted caramel layer, then refrigerate for 2–3 hours to let it set.

TOPPING

Cocoa powder, sea salt, chocolate scrolls

Dust with cocoa powder if desired, and sprinkle with sea salt. Garnish with chocolate scrolls.

WHAT IF?

If buckwheat flour is unavailable, you can use wholewheat flour or all-purpose flour instead. This recipe works well with quinoa flour too.

Chocolate & Strawberry
MOUSSE SILK TART

🍴 MAKES ONE 8 INCH TART

One of my many phases in dessert-making was when I discovered agar agar on popular demand as a vegan alternative to gelatine. I luckily used just enough to set the filling, allowing neat slices which turned out refreshingly light and delicious. This is an airy tart, mousse-like and smooth as silk.

INGREDIENTS

TART BASE

125 g digestive biscuits
75 g whole almonds
60 g clarified butter/ghee, melted, cooled

CHOCOLATE PANNA COTTA FILLING

250 ml cream
125 ml milk, warm
1 tbsp cocoa powder
2–3 tbsp brown sugar
3/4 tsp agar agar
100 g dark chocolate, chopped fine
100 g strawberries, chopped

TOPPING

Fresh berries, chocolate shards, fresh mint

METHOD

Lightly grease an 8 inch loose-bottomed tart tin.
Place digestive biscuits and almonds in a processor and blend to a fine meal.
Alternatively, a dry grinder will work. Work in short pulses.
Stir in melted clarified butter/ghee.
Work up the sides of a tart tin, then press firmly to make the base.
Place in the freezer for 30 minutes while you make the chocolate filling.

Place the cream, milk, cocoa powder, sugar and agar agar in a heavy-bottomed saucepan and whisk to a smooth mix with a balloon whisk.
Stir in the chocolate.
Place over medium heat and bring to a rolling boil, stirring constantly.
Reduce the heat to a low simmer, and continue to cook for another 4–5 minutes, whisking constantly.
Cool to tepid, whisking now and then to keep the cream uniform and to prevent a film from forming on top.

ASSEMBLY

Scatter the chopped strawberries over the base of the chilled tart base.
Gently pour over the filling, and leave to set in the fridge overnight.
Garnish with fresh fruit, chocolate shavings, etc.

*(**Note:** The potency of agar agar sometimes differs across brands.)*

WHAT IF?

If you don't have agar agar, you can use gelatine instead.

Stovetop Walnut Brownie
WHOLEGRAIN TART

MAKES ONE 8 INCH TART

Wholegrain, no refined sugar, eggless and delicious! Did I tell you it's a one-bowl recipe too? This was another experiment in a series of stovetop or no-oven and no-egg baking during the pandemic lockdown, and I really enjoyed it. On the occasions I couldn't get condensed milk in those trying times, I used yogurt, which was easier to source.

There is a certain magic that gets created when you heat ghee and whisk in jaggery powder or brown sugar. It heightens the earthy flavours, adding almost butterscotch notes, making the bake quite addictive. The first time I experienced this was while making Anzacs a couple of years ago and have since enjoyed using the method.

I've baked these in a heavy-bottomed cast iron vessel or Dutch oven with a tight-fitting lid, and in a tart tin.

INGREDIENTS

DRY MIX

100 g wholewheat flour
1 tsp baking powder
½ tsp baking soda
A pinch of salt
50 g walnuts, chopped
50 g dark chocolate chips

WET MIX

100 g clarified butter/ghee
175 g jaggery powder
35 g cocoa powder
125 g thick yogurt
1 tsp vanilla extract

METHOD

Place a trivet in a Dutch oven (or any heavy-bottomed vessel), and place it on the stovetop/gas with the lid on and leave to heat on simmer. Line the base of an 8 inch loose-bottomed tart tin with parchment paper. Grease the sides lightly with a brush (or the fingertips).

Whisk together the dry ingredients in a small bowl. Reserve.

Heat the ghee till tepid and pour into a large bowl. Whisk in the jaggery powder and cocoa powder until smooth and fragrant. Whisk in the yogurt and vanilla extract.

Now fold in the dry ingredients. Don't over-mix.

Transfer the mix to the prepared tart tin and top with walnut halves and chocolate chips, if desired.

Quickly take the lid off the Dutch oven, place the tart tin on the trivet/rack. Be careful since the vessel will be very hot.

Return the lid and simmer over low heat, covered, for 25 minutes.

Turn the heat off and leave it in the vessel for another 5–7 minutes.

TOPPING

Walnut halves, chocolate chips

Take off the lid and take the tart tin out once it's cool enough to handle. Cool completely, and refrigerate until cold before slicing.

(***Note:*** *Do make sure the tart tin fits into the vessel before heating. This can be made in a round 8 inch tin too.*)

WHAT IF?

If you're using an oven, bake in a preheated oven at 180°C for 20–25 minutes.

Bittersweet Chocolate Espresso
TART

🍴 MAKES ONE 14 INCH LONG TART

Another simple tart, because often no celebration at our place is complete without a hint of coffee. The tart base is an adaptation of an eggless gingerbread man I made one Christmas. I've played with that recipe, which has all the goodness of wholewheat flour, coconut sugar, honey, crystallized ginger, and my favourite ingredient: ghee. I had the most fun piping these free-hand Christmas trees with melted chocolate, then adding little dragees to them.

Use instant coffee powder instead of espresso powder, or your favourite tart base recipe if you like, or else a biscuit base, but make this, you must!

INGREDIENTS

TART BASE

75 g clarified butter/ghee, room temperature
45 g coconut sugar
1 tsp espresso powder
A pinch of salt
½ tsp baking soda
140 g wholewheat flour
2 tbsp honey
2–3 tbsp cream

MASCARPONE ESPRESSO FILLING

200 g mascarpone
100 ml cream
30 g coconut sugar
1 tbsp espresso powder

METHOD

Preheat the oven to 180°C. Line the base of a 14 inch rectangular loose-bottomed tart tin with a strip of parchment paper. Alternatively, use a round 8 inch tart tin.

In the bowl of a stand mixer, whisk the clarified butter/ghee and coconut sugar until smooth. Then add the espresso powder, salt and baking soda. Whisk.
Alternatively, use a large bowl and an electric hand-mixer.
Now add the wholewheat flour and mix on low speed until just combined. Drizzle over the honey, then add just enough cream to bring the base together. The dough should hold when pinched between the fingertips.
Push into the tart tin, building up the sides first, then firmly pat into the base.
Bake for 12–15 minutes until firm to the touch. Cool completely on the cooling rack.

(**Note:** The tart base can be made a day before.)

Place all the ingredients in a large bowl and whisk just until smooth. Don't overbeat. We're looking for a thick filling that holds well.

CHOCOLATE ESPRESSO TOPPING

100 g bittersweet chocolate, chopped fine
150 ml cream
2 tbsp honey
1 tsp espresso powder

TOPPING

50 g dark chocolate, melted

Place the chocolate in a glass bowl.
Heat the cream till hot but not boiling and pour over the chocolate. Allow to stand for 10–15 minutes until the chocolate softens. Add the honey and espresso powder, and stir gently until smooth. Cool.

ASSEMBLE

Assemble the tart by filling the shell with the mascarpone espresso cream. Using an offset spatula, spread it evenly, then top with the chocolate espresso filling. Leave to set in the fridge for a few hours, or overnight.
Garnish as desired with melted chocolate shapes.

Mocha

TARTOOKIE

MAKES ONE 8 INCH TART

A coffee and chocolate cookie tart is simple comfort food in my book. This is a twist to the cookie-for-one recipe (page 113). While attempting to bake a big batch of that recipe, I crossed paths with a tart tin lying on the kitchen counter. The cookie plans changed suddenly and we soon had a tartookie (as christened by my friend Ruchira), or a cookie in a tart tin.

As usual, the magic that is created when hot ghee meets brown sugar won me over. The top is just chocolate chips scattered over the hot tartookie as it steps out of the oven. It yielded a thin, glossy cover that held the cocoa nibs beautifully.

INGREDIENTS

DRY MIX

120 g wholewheat flour
60 g quick-cooking oats
1 tbsp instant coffee powder
A pinch of salt
1 tsp baking powder
½ tsp baking soda
50 g dark chocolate chips

WET MIX

1 chia egg (1 tbsp chia seeds + 3 tbsp water)
100 g brown sugar
100 g clarified butter/ghee

TOPPING

50 g dark chocolate, chopped
2 tbsp cocoa nibs

METHOD

Lightly grease an 8 inch loose-bottomed tart tin.

Whisk together the dry ingredients in a small bowl. Reserve.

In a small bowl, stir together the water and chia seeds. Leave to stand for 5 minutes to gel while you mix the other ingredients.

Place the brown sugar in a large bowl. Heat the clarified butter/ghee and pour over the brown sugar. Whisk well, and then stir in the chia egg.

Add the dry mix to the wet mix, and stir well to combine.

Transfer the dough-like batter to the prepared tin.

Place in a cold oven. Bake at 170°C for 30 minutes.

Cool on a rack for 10 minutes. Gently loosen the tart sides by pushing up the base but keep the tartookie in the tin by gently moving it back into place.

Scatter the top with the dark chocolate. It should melt soon. Spread with the offset spatula.

Sprinkle cocoa nibs or chocolate non-pareils, etc. Cool completely, then slice and serve.

*(**Note:** If the weather is warm, refrigerate for 30 minutes for the chocolate to set.)*

Dark Chocolate

WHOLEWHEAT ALMOND TARTS

🍴 MAKES SIX 3 INCH TARTS

I created these for a V-Day campaign themed 'love yourself', dabbling in things I enjoy—food, baking, chocolate, vintage props, rose petals and moody frames. The tart is dead easy to bring together. I piped the filling since it adds charm to desserts. You could simply spoon the filling into the shells if you like.

INGREDIENTS

TART BASE

100 g wholewheat flour
50 g whole almonds
½ tsp baking soda
A pinch of salt
50 g clarified butter/ghee, melted, cooled
50 g coconut sugar
100 g dark chocolate, chopped fine

CHOCOLATE FILLING

175 g dark chocolate, chopped fine
215 ml cream

TOPPING

Seasonal fruit, organic rose petals, chocolate shards

METHOD

Place all the ingredients for the base in the jar of a mixer/grinder.
Blend to a fine meal.
The dough should come together when pinched between the fingertips.
Lightly grease six 3 inch loose-bottomed tart tins. Divide the dough between them, pushing up the sides and into the bottom to make the tart base.
Put the tart tins on a cookie tray and place it in the freezer while you preheat the oven to 170°C.
Bake the bases for about 15–20 minutes.
Cool completely in the tins.

Place the chocolate in a glass bowl.
Heat the cream till hot but not boiling and pour over the chocolate.
Allow to stand for 10–15 minutes until the chocolate softens, then stir gently until smooth. Repeat twice after every 20 minutes.
Once it begins to hold form, either place it in a piping bag fitted with a star nozzle and pipe rosettes, else divide and fill the tart bases equally.
Top with seasonal fruit, chocolate shards, organic rose petals, etc.

Roasted Beetroot & Chocolate
WALNUT BLENDER TART

MAKES ONE 8 INCH TART

A new experiment, a tart which turned out different from all my other tarts, bringing together my love for chocolate and for experimenting with vegetables in desserts. While I've created several desserts with pumpkin, it had been a while since I used beets. This tart reignited my love for beets in dessert.

The filling turned out really moist, refreshingly different, with subtle, earthy undertones from the sweetness of roasted beets. The only downside is that it doesn't keep for too long because of the moistness of the beets. Hence, it's best finished in twenty-four hours, but then again, ours didn't last that long!

INGREDIENTS

TART BASE

75 g digestive biscuits, broken
50 g walnuts
50 g unsalted butter, melted, cooled

FILLING

200 ml cream
125 g bittersweet chocolate, chopped fine
2 tbsp brown sugar
150 g roasted beetroot (1 small)
1½ tbsp cornflour
1 tbsp Cointreau (optional)

CHOCOLATE GANACHE

85 g dark chocolate, chopped fine
100 ml cream

METHOD

Place the biscuits and walnuts in the jar of a mixer/grinder. Blend to a fine meal.
Stir in the melted butter.
Press into an 8 inch loose-bottomed tart tin and place in the freezer while you make the filling.
Preheat the oven to 180°C.

Blend all the ingredients for the filling together in a high-powered blender.
Transfer the filling into the chilled biscuit base in the tart tin.
Bake in a preheated oven at 180°C for 30 minutes. Cool completely, then refrigerate overnight.
Pipe over the ganache. Garnish with fresh seasonal berries, and dust with dehydrated beetroot powder.
This is best consumed within a day.

Place the chocolate in a glass bowl.
Heat the cream till hot but not boiling and pour over the chocolate.
Allow to stand for 10–15 minutes until the chocolate softens, then stir gently until smooth. Repeat twice every 20 minutes. Once it begins to hold form, transfer it to a piping bag fitted with a star nozzle and pipe a few rosettes over the top.

Dark Chocolate & Pumpkin
WALNUT TART

🍴 MAKES ONE 8 INCH TART

A delicious wholegrain tart packed with walnuts, which can go vegan with a few changes. It's a really great way to sneak veggies into dessert; unsuspecting folk, especially kids, will never pick up on it! The puree is from the yellow pumpkin, or our humble kaddu, as it's locally known, and is available all year round.

INGREDIENTS

TART BASE

75 g digestive biscuits
50 g toasted walnuts
50 g clarified butter/ghee, melted, cooled

CHOCOLATE PUMPKIN FILLING

200 g bittersweet chocolate, chopped fine
50 ml cream
100 g fresh pumpkin purée (page 264)
Zest of **1** orange
2 tbsp maple syrup
1 tbsp walnut butter
1 tsp garam masala (page 267)

TOPPING

Dark chocolate shavings, walnut halves

METHOD

Place the biscuits and walnuts in the jar of a mixer/grinder. Blend to a fine meal.
Stir in the melted butter.
Turn into an 8 inch loose-bottomed tart tin, working the sides up first, and then the base.
Place the base in the freezer for 15 minutes while you preheat the oven to 180°C.
Bake the base for 10 minutes and move to a cooling rack. Leave the oven on.
In the meantime, prepare the filling.

Place the chocolate in a glass bowl. Heat the cream till hot but not boiling and pour over the chocolate. Allow to stand for 10–15 minutes until the chocolate softens, then stir gently until smooth.
Whisk in the remaining ingredients for the filling.
Add the chocolate pumpkin filling to the tart base and level with an offset spatula.
Bake at 180°C for 20 minutes, then leave to cool in the oven.
Refrigerate until set. Grate over with dark chocolate and top with walnut halves.

WHAT IF?

If you don't have walnut butter, you can use any nut butter instead.

Dark Chocolate & Strawberry
RUSTIC CRUMBLE

MAKES ONE 6-7 INCH CRUMBLE

A fruit crumble is a dessert I have always loved, yet surprisingly I never found a chocolate one I liked. That changed with this indulgent rustic bake from my sweet friend Parul, the super talented chef at Music & Mountains in Delhi. As large-hearted as she is, she shared the recipe as soon as I requested her. It has two of my favourite ingredients under a crisp, buttery topping: strawberries and dark chocolate.

In the oven in under 15 minutes, this is the quickest fruit and chocolate dessert you can bake! Our first batch of harvested homegrown strawberries went into this, and though not technically a tart, I just had to share it!

INGREDIENTS

FILLING

250 g strawberries, halved
200 g dark chocolate, roughly chopped

CRUMBLE TOPPING

75 g butter, softened
100 g all purpose flour
100 g vanilla sugar (page 262)

METHOD

Preheat the oven to 200°C.
Stir together the strawberries and chocolate in a bowl. Transfer to a baking dish.

Mix the topping ingredients together with a fork to make a breadcrumb-textured mix.
Top the fruit and chocolate mix with the crumble and bake for approximately 25–30 minutes, until the top is golden brown.
Serve warm, perhaps with a scoop of vanilla ice-cream!

Christmas Brownie

TART

☗ MAKES ONE 8 INCH TART

Bake your favourite brownie batter in a tart tin, then top it with a nice, rich chocolate ganache, dress it up with fresh berries, and quite simply, you have a festive dessert! The holiday season tends to bring out my creative best. The charm of tarts has been at an all-time high for me over the last year or so. From cookies to brownies, everything seemed to go the tart way.

INGREDIENTS

BROWNIE TART

75 g unsalted butter, softened
75 g dark chocolate, chopped fine
100 g soaked fruit mince, chopped
100 g walnuts, chopped
25 g cocoa powder
75 g wholewheat flour
A pinch of salt
1 tsp vanilla extract
75 g Greek yogurt (or thick yogurt)
100 g brown sugar

ORANGE CHOCOLATE GANACHE

100 g dark chocolate, chopped fine
150 ml cream
Zest of **1** orange

TOPPING
Seasonal berries

METHOD

Preheat the oven to 180°C. Lightly grease an 8 inch loose-bottomed tart tin.

Place the chocolate and butter in a glass bowl and melt using the double-boiler method or in the microwave for 30 seconds.
Transfer the melted chocolate mixture to the bowl of a stand mixer with the remaining ingredients for the brownie tart.
Alternatively, use a large bowl and an electric hand-mixer.
Stir at a low speed until just combined.
Turn into the prepared tart tin and push into place, levelling out as required.
Bake for 20 minutes, until slightly firm to the touch.
Cool completely in the tin, then loosen the sides and return the tart to the tin.
Top the tart with the orange chocolate ganache and leave to set in the fridge for 30 minutes.
Garnish with berries if you like.

Place the chocolate in a glass bowl. Heat the cream till hot but not boiling and pour over the chocolate. Allow to stand for 10–15 minutes until the chocolate softens, then add the zest and stir gently until smooth. Repeat twice after every 20 minutes. Cool to a spreadable consistency.

Dark Chocolate & Fresh Cherry

DATE WALNUT TARTS
(NO-BAKE, GLUTEN-FREE)

MAKES FOUR 3 INCH TARTS

These are simple, no-bake tarts that came about when high temperatures were roasting us in the plains of north India last summer. At 46°C, sweet little bites like these make the heat somewhat more bearable!

INGREDIENTS

METHOD

TART BASE

75 g dates, pitted
50 g walnuts
50 g dark chocolate, chopped fine

Place all the ingredients in the jar of a food processor and process until the dough comes together.

Press into four 3 inch loose-bottomed tart tins. Place in the freezer for about an hour.

WHIPPED VANILLA-CREAM FILLING

200 g cream cheese, chilled
100 g mascarpone, chilled
2 tbsp brown sugar
¼ scraped vanilla bean
3 tbsp fruit preserves

With an electric hand-beater, whisk the cream cheese, mascarpone, sugar and scraped vanilla bean until smooth.

Divide the fruit preserve over the tart bases, then top with the whipped vanilla cream filling.
Garnish with fresh berries, sprigs of thyme and dark chocolate shards. Refrigerate for 2–3 hours before serving.

*(**Note:** Use any fruit in season and make these. They are quick and taste great!)*

TOPPING

Fresh berries, thyme, chocolate shards

Dark Chocolate & Coffee
WALNUT TART

Chocolate and coffee are meant to be together. They bring out the best in each other, and often the happy in me! I made this for World Chocolate Day with the two flavours I absolutely love. A whipped dark chocolate and coffee ganache nested luxuriously in a coffee walnut biscuit base. Need I say more?

INGREDIENTS

COFFEE WALNUT BISCUIT BASE

125 g digestive biscuits
75 g walnuts
1 tsp coffee powder
50 g clarified butter/ghee melted, cooled

WHIPPED DARK CHOCOLATE COFFEE FILLING

200 g dark chocolate, chopped fine
250 ml cream
1 tbsp instant coffee powder

METHOD

Place the biscuits, walnuts and coffee powder in the jar of a mixer/grinder. Blend to a fine meal.
Stir in the ghee.
Turn into an 8 inch loose-bottomed tart tin, working the sides up first, and then the base.
Place the base in the freezer, while the filling is prepared.

Place the chocolate in a glass bowl. Heat the cream till hot but not boiling and pour over the chocolate. Allow to stand for 10–15 minutes until the chocolate softens, then add the coffee and stir gently until smooth. Repeat twice after every 20 minutes.
Refrigerate for 30 minutes until it just begins to get a little firm, then whip on high speed until it's light and changes colour.

ASSEMBLE

Take the tart tin out of the freezer. Push out the base very gently to loosen the shell. Return to the tin.
Transfer the whipped filling into the base and level it with an offset spatula. Garnish with chocolate dragees, etc., if desired.
Refrigerate for at least 4 hours or overnight until firm.

Coconut Milk & Chocolate
MOUSSE TART

MAKES ONE 8 INCH TART

This tart came together quite simply one morning while playing with the ingredients on hand. I'm a huge fan of using nuts in tart bases, and this time I added some chocolate as well. Oats, walnuts, chocolate and ghee make for a delicious base, one good enough to eat on its own! I love the texture it adds to the otherwise smooth coconut milk chocolate filling, deeply delicious in every way.

INGREDIENTS

TART BASE

100 g quick-cooking oats
50 g walnuts
50 g dark chocolate, chopped
15 g brown sugar
25 g clarified butter/ghee

COCONUT MILK CHOCOLATE CREAM

1½ tsp gelatine powder
2 tbsp warm water
250 ml coconut milk
100 ml cream
100 g dark chocolate, chopped fine
15 g cocoa powder
40 g brown sugar
A pinch of salt
2 tbsp corn flour

TOPPING

Chocolate confectionary, non-pareils, fresh cherries

METHOD

Place all the ingredients for the base in the jar of the processor/blender. Blend to a coarse consistency in short pulses. The mixture should hold together when pressed between the fingertips.
Turn into an 8 inch loose-bottomed tart tin, working the sides up first, and then the base.
Put the tart tin in the freezer while the oven preheats.
Preheat the oven to 180°C.
Bake the base for 12–15 minutes, then cool on the rack while the filling is prepared.
Loosen the base gently once cooled, and leave it in the tin.

Sprinkle the gelatine over the water in a small bowl and leave until spongy. Place the bowl in warm water and leave until the gelatine is clear.
Place the remaining ingredients except the chocolate in a heavy-bottomed saucepan. Whisk to mix. Stir in the chocolate.
Place over low heat and bring to a simmer, stirring constantly, until the mixture thickens to the consistency of custard.
Take off the heat and stir in the bloomed gelatine mixture. Whisk well to mix.
Strain the gelatine mixture into this. Whisk well to mix.
Strain into a bowl, then cool for about 30 minutes, whisking a couple of times in between.
Pour into the baked, cooled tart base.
Cover and refrigerate overnight to set.

Top with chocolate confectionary, chocolate non-pareils and fresh cherries.

Chocolate & Blueberry
WHOLEGRAIN TARTS

⚌ MAKES EIGHT 3 INCH TARTS

Rustic little tarts, as pretty as can be. Made with a wholegrain buckwheat tart base, the filling is sensuous, smooth dark chocolate. Fresh blueberries, chocolate shavings, a dusting of cocoa powder, and a hint of mint completed them. Quality ingredients, simple procedures, good garnish and eye-catching presentation all make for good dessert!

INGREDIENTS

TART BASE
DRY MIX

100 g wholewheat flour
50 g buckwheat flour
½ tsp baking soda
A pinch of salt

WET MIX

100 g unsalted butter, softened
100 g brown sugar
1 tsp vanilla extract
125 g dark chocolate, ground/
chopped fine

DARK CHOCOLATE FILLING

240 g dark chocolate chopped
fine
350 ml cream
30 g clarified butter/ghee
1 tbsp honey

TOPPING

Cocoa powder, chocolate
shards, fresh blueberries and
sprigs of fresh mint.

METHOD

Whisk together the dry ingredients in a small bowl. Reserve.

In the bowl of a stand mixer, whisk butter, sugar and vanilla for 3–4 minutes on medium speed until smooth.
Alternatively, use a large bowl and an electric hand-mixer.
Stir in the ground chocolate and dry mix on the lowest speed, just enough for the dough to come together. Don't over-mix, else the cookies will become hard.
Bring the dough together, then divide between the tart tins, working the sides up first, and then the base.
Place the tart tins on a tray in the freezer while you preheat the oven.
Preheat the oven to 170°C.
Bake the tart bases for 12–15 minutes until just firm to the touch.
Cool completely in the tart tins on the cookie rack.

Place the chocolate in a glass bowl.
Heat the cream till hot but not boiling and pour over the chocolate.
Allow to stand for 10–15 minutes until the chocolate softens, then add the clarified butter/ghee and honey, then stir gently until smooth.
Repeat twice after every 20 minutes.
Spoon into the tart tins and refrigerate for 1–2 hours, until set.

Sift over the cocoa powder. Garnish with chocolate shards, fresh blueberries and sprigs of fresh mint.

Quintessential Amul
TART (NO-BAKE)

MAKES ONE 8 INCH TART

Growing up in India, our childhoods were partially measured in spoons of all sorts of special deliciousness. Among favourites were brands like Bournvita, Amul butter, Mother Dairy ice-cream, 5-Star chocolate, Bru coffee, names that still add deep nostalgia to those memories.

I had a few slabs of Amul dark chocolate on hand one day, a reasonably good 55% dark chocolate with packaging to match. Some of it went into this tart, the childhood connect perhaps making it sweeter!

The tart is as simple as it is delicious. If you don't have the time or patience to pipe ganache over, possibly top it with fruit or candied nuts, maybe praline.

INGREDIENTS

TART BASE

120 g digestive biscuits
1 tbsp brown sugar
50 g walnuts
40 g clarified butter/ghee, melted, cooled

FILLING

250 g Amul Tanzania chocolate bar, chopped fine
200 ml cream

WHIPPED CHOCOLATE GANACHE

125 g Amul Tanzania chocolate bar, chopped fine
100 ml cream

METHOD

Place all the ingredients for the base in a processor and blend to a breadcrumb-like consistency.
Turn into an 8 inch loose-bottomed tart tin, working the sides up first, and then the base.
Place in the freezer for about 30 minutes, then gently loosen the tart base and return to the tin.

Place the chocolate in a glass bowl. Heat the cream till hot but not boiling and pour over the chocolate. Allow to stand for 10–15 minutes until the chocolate softens, then stir gently until smooth. Repeat twice after every 20 minutes.
Once it gets cool and is still pourable, pour into the tart base and level out using an offset spatula. Refrigerate for 30 minutes, then pipe the whipped ganache over the filling.

Place the chocolate in a glass bowl. Heat the cream till hot but not boiling and pour over the chocolate. Allow to stand for 10–15 minutes until the chocolate softens, then stir gently until smooth. Repeat twice after every 20 minutes.
Place into the fridge until slightly firm, then use an electric hand-blender and whip until it's light and changes colour slightly. Transfer to a piping bag fitted with a star nozzle and pipe over the chocolate filling. Refrigerate for at least an hour.

Nutella & Fresh Cherry

TART

🍴 **MAKES ONE 8 INCH TART**

Another rare instance where I use Nutella, yet this one is so worth it. It's a remake of a tart I made several years ago for a baking challenge for the Daring Bakers, a group that I was part of. Those years of my life challenged the baker in me and introduced me to a wider world of desserts. This tart is filled with a combination of fresh cherries, deeply luscious dark chocolate, and Nutella. I topped it with cherries since I've always made the tart in summer.

INGREDIENTS

BISCUIT BASE

150 g digestive biscuits
1 tbsp cocoa powder
50 g clarified butter/ghee, melted, cooled

CHOCOLATE FILLING

400 ml cream, room temperature
2 tbsp cornflour
150 g bittersweet chocolate, chopped fine
75 g Nutella

TOPPING

200 g balsamic cherries (page 259)
A few sprigs of fresh mint

METHOD

Preheat the oven to 180°C. Lightly grease an 8 inch loose-bottomed tart tin.

Place the biscuits and cocoa powder in the jar of a mixer/grinder and blend to a fine meal.
Alternatively, place biscuits in a Ziploc bag and crush with a rolling pin to make crumbs. Stir in the cocoa powder.
Stir in the ghee. Turn into the prepared tin, working the sides up first, and then the base.
Bake the biscuit base for 20 minutes.
Cool completely on the rack. It will firm up as it cools.
Once cool, loosen the base and leave it in the tart tin.

For the filling, begin by stirring the cornflour into 50 ml cream. Reserve.
Place the remaining cream, chocolate and Nutella in a heavy-bottomed saucepan. Simmer over low heat until the chocolate melts, stirring constantly.
Slowly whisk in the reserved cream and cornflour mix, and continue to stir until the mixture thickens to a batter-like texture, thicker than flowing custard.
Cool for about 30 minutes, stirring once in a while.
Scatter the pitted cherries over the cooled tart base.
Pour the cooled filling over the cherries. Refrigerate for 3–4 hours, or overnight until the filling is set.
Top the tart with the balsamic cherries and garnish with fresh mint.

Bittersweet Chocolate
SABLÉ COOKIE TART

🍴 MAKES ONE 8 INCH TART

Last but not the least, another recipe where a batch of cookie dough found its way into one of my most used baking tins: the 8 inch tart tin. Quite often when I set off to bake cookies, diving deep into my blog to rediscover old gems, the cookie dough finds its way into a tart tin.

This tart was made on one such morning while I was attempting to redo chocolate pretzel cookies. This was way faster than baking cookies, and so fuss-free. Personally, I think it's quite fun to rethink cookie dough in different avatars. I also enjoyed giving my piping skills some practice! You'll find a recipe for a chocolate lattice on page 252.

INGREDIENTS

DRY MIX

100 g all purpose flour
50 g whole wheat flour
¼ tsp baking soda

WET MIX

125 g unsalted butter, softened
125 g bittersweet chocolate
100 g brown sugar
1 tbsp instant coffee powder
½ tsp vanilla extract
A pinch of salt

GANACHE TOPPING

60 g bittersweet chocolate
100 g cream

METHOD

Preheat the oven to 180°C.

Whisk together the dry mix in a bowl. Reserve.

Place the chocolate and butter in a large bowl and melt using the double-boiler method or in the microwave, 30 seconds at a time. Whisk until smooth.
Whisk in the brown sugar, followed by the coffee powder, vanilla extract and salt.
Gently fold in the reserved dry mix.
Transfer the cookie dough to a 8 inch loose-bottomed tart tin and spread uniformly.
Bake for 25–30 minutes until the dough is slightly firm to the touch in the centre.
Cool completely on the cooling rack.

Place the chocolate in a glass bowl. Heat the cream till hot but not boiling and pour over the chocolate. Allow to stand for 10–15 minutes until the chocolate softens, and stir gently until smooth. Cool to a spreadable consistency and spread over the cooled tart.
Top with piped chocolate decorations, fresh berries etc.
Slice with a heavy sharp knife.

Cupcakes, Traybakes & Brownies

Quick and delicious cupcakes, traybakes and brownies are ideal for those who are just beginning to try their hand at baking. These recipes are pretty much what you can call bake-and-serve. Play with flavours, swirl them with toppings—from drop-dead simple ones to super indulgent delights, you can have it all!

Dark Chocolate

WHOLEWHEAT BROWNIES

🍴 MAKES 16 SQUARES

Decadent wholewheat dark chocolate brownies, just right for a spot of indulgence. Since they are wholewheat, they are less 'guilt-ridden', and the use of olive oil instead of butter convinces you to reach for more.

INGREDIENTS

DRY MIX

75 g wholewheat flour
1 tsp baking powder
A pinch of salt
50 g dark chocolate chips
50 g toasted almonds, chopped

WET MIX

65 g unsalted butter, softened
35 ml light olive oil
100 g dark chocolate, chopped
100 g brown sugar
2 eggs
1 tsp vanilla extract

METHOD

Preheat the oven to 180°C. Line a square 8 x 8 inch baking tin with parchment paper.

Whisk together the dry ingredients in a small bowl. Reserve.

Place the butter, olive oil and chocolate in a large bowl and melt, either in the microwave, 30 seconds at a time, or using the double-boiler method. Whisk until smooth.
Whisk in the sugar, followed by the eggs and vanilla extract.
Now fold in the dry mix.
Turn the batter into the prepared tin and bake for 18–20 minutes. Cool completely in the tin, then remove gently and cut into squares using a sharp knife.

The Best Chocolate
CUPCAKES (EGGLESS)

MAKES 6

Some recipes give you much happiness by just sharing them, and these cupcakes fall into that bracket. I got amazing feedback from so many who baked them, enough to safely call them the best wholegrain cupcakes ever!

INGREDIENTS

DRY MIX

75 g wholewheat flour
1½ tbsp cocoa powder
½ tsp baking soda
¼ tsp baking powder
¼ tsp salt

WET MIX

100 g brown sugar
50 g clarified butter/ghee, melted, cooled
1 tsp vanilla extract
35 g Greek yogurt
60 ml brewed coffee
½ tbsp white vinegar

CHOCOLATE GANACHE FROSTING

150 g dark chocolate, chopped fine
225 ml cream

METHOD

Preheat the oven to 180°C. Line a 12-cavity muffin tray with 6 liners.

Whisk together the dry ingredients in a small bowl. Reserve.

In a large bowl, whisk together the ingredients for the wet mix until homogeneous.
Fold the reserved dry mix into the wet mix until just combined.
Divide between cupcake liners. Bake for 25–30 minutes until done or a toothpick tester comes out clean. Cool completely on a cooling rack, and frost if desired.

Place the chocolate in a glass bowl.
Heat the cream till hot but not boiling and pour over the chocolate.
Allow to stand for 10–15 minutes until the chocolate softens, then stir gently until smooth. Repeat twice after every 20 minutes until it reaches piping consistency.
Once the cupcakes are cool, and the frosting the desired consistency, pipe it on with a star nozzle.

Bakery-Style Banana Chocolate
WHOLEGRAIN MUFFINS (EGGLESS)

🍴 MAKES 4 LARGE OR 6 REGULAR

Yet another delightful twist to one of my most popular recipes, and it's a simple no-brainer recipe too. I've baked it into a banana loaf, into cupcakes (inspired by my friend Sonalini), into banana caramel dessert jars, and now these. I often play with the recipe and it never disappoints. I hope you enjoy these as much as we do!

INGREDIENTS

DRY MIX

45 g quick cooking oats
60 g wholewheat flour
45 g coconut sugar
¼ tsp baking soda
½ tsp baking powder
½ tsp cinnamon powder
A pinch of salt
30 g dark chocolate chips

WET MIX

75 g bananas or **1** large, ripe banana, mashed
2 tbsp light olive oil
50 g Greek yogurt
1 tsp vanilla extract

METHOD

Preheat the oven to 180°C. Line a muffin tray with 4 or 6 liners, as required.

Whisk together the dry ingredients in a small bowl. Reserve.

In a large bowl, mash the banana with a fork. Stir in the oil, yogurt and vanilla extract.

Fold the reserved dry mix into the wet mix until just combined. Do not over-mix.

Divide between the muffin liners, and bake for about 25–30 minutes, until the top is firm to the touch and a toothpick tester comes out clean. Serve warm or at room temperature.

WHAT IF?

If you don't have a 6 cavity muffin tray, you can use a 12 cavity one.
Place muffin liners in 6 and fill the empty compartments with a little water to aid even baking.

Quinoa Cocoa
BROWNIES

🍴 MAKES 16 SQUARES

This is another recipe from my 'discovery of quinoa' phase. Being a content creator for brands comes with its own perks, the greatest being the opportunity to explore new ingredients. When quinoa took the world by storm, India began cultivating its own crop. Quite soon, there were several homegrown brands available and I was excited to work with some of them. This recipe is from a time when I did a ton of recipes with this pseudo cereal. Quite interestingly, cooked quinoa added a nice texture to my bakes.

INGREDIENTS

75 g clarified butter/ghee, melted, cooled
200 g brown sugar
90 g cooked red quinoa, cooled
2 eggs
60 g thick yogurt
60 g cocoa powder
½ tsp baking soda
1 tsp baking powder
⅛ tsp salt

METHOD

Preheat the oven to 180°C. Line an 8 x 8 inch loose-bottomed baking tin with parchment paper.

Place all ingredients in the bowl of a food processor. Process on high speed for 10–15 seconds until well blended.

Turn the batter into the prepared tin.

Bake for 30–35 minutes until a toothpick tester comes out with a few moist crumbs hanging.

Cool completely in the tin, then refrigerate for a few hours before slicing.

*(**Note:** This recipe will need a food processor.)*

Bakery-Style Chocolate Orange
WHOLEWHEAT MUFFINS (EGGLESS)

MAKES 4 BAKERY-STYLE MUFFINS

Like I had a 'make everything with quinoa' phase, I also had a 'bake everything eggless' phase. Talk about self-motivation, this was a phase of rediscovery and untold joy. Joy for the followers of my blog and Instagram handle too because they are always so happy to see an eggless recipe. This is for all of those who inspire me to push my boundaries, a cupcake recipe that can only be described as soul satisfying.

INGREDIENTS

DRY MIX

75 g wholewheat flour
30 g cocoa powder
A pinch of salt
½ tsp baking powder
⅛ tsp baking soda
50 g walnuts, chopped
50 g dark chocolate chips

WET MIX

50 g clarified butter/ghee, warm
75 g jaggery powder
1 chia egg (1 tbsp chia + 3 tbsp water)
1 tbsp bitter orange marmalade
50 ml buttermilk

METHOD

Preheat the oven to 180°C. Line a 4-cupcake mould with liners.

Sift the flour, cocoa powder, salt, baking powder and baking soda. Stir in the walnuts and chocolate chips. Reserve in a small bowl.

In a small bowl, stir together the water and chia seeds. Leave to stand for 5 minutes to gel while you mix the other ingredients.
In a large bowl, whisk together the warm ghee and jaggery powder, followed by the chia egg and the marmalade.
Stir in half the dry mix and half the buttermilk. Repeat.
Divide between the muffin liners.
Bake for 25 minutes, until the top is firm to the touch and a toothpick tester comes out clean.

Cocoa Walnut

WHOLEWHEAT BROWNIES (EGGLESS)

MAKES 16 SQUARES

These are the simplest brownies you'll ever make. Delicious, fudgy, wholegrain and in the oven in under 20 minutes. Need I say more?

INGREDIENTS

DRY MIX

65 g all-purpose flour
60 g wholewheat flour
50 g cocoa powder
200 g coconut sugar
1 tsp baking soda
A pinch of salt
50 g walnuts, chopped
50 g dark chocolate chips

WET MIX

75 g clarified butter/ghee
225 ml buttermilk
½ tsp vanilla extract

TOPPING

Chocolate chips

METHOD

Preheat oven to 180°C. Line an 8 x 8 inch baking tin with parchment paper.

Whisk together the dry ingredients in a small bowl. Reserve.

In a large bowl, whisk together the ghee, buttermilk and vanilla essence.
Fold the reserved dry mix into the wet mix until just combined to make a smooth, lump-free batter. Don't over-mix.
Transfer to the prepared tin, and scatter over with chocolate chips.
Bake for about 20–25 minutes, until a toothpick tester comes out clean.
Cool completely, then refrigerate for a couple of hours before cutting.

Almond Oat Salted Caramel
BARS (EGGLESS)

MAKES 16 SQUARES

Inspired by a favourite cookie, the Anzac, these simple bars are packed with oats and almonds. It's one of the rare instances that I use Nutella, and it's well worth it!

INGREDIENTS

DRY MIX

100 g whole almonds
50 g brown sugar
100 g all-purpose flour
1 tsp baking soda
100 g quick-cooking oats

WET MIX

100 g clarified butter/ghee, melted, room temperature
100 g salted caramel sauce (page 255)

TOPPING

200 g Nutella
Cocoa powder for dusting
Slivered almonds to garnish

METHOD

Preheat the oven to 170°C. Line an 8 x 8 inch baking tin with parchment paper.

Run the almonds, flour, brown sugar and baking soda in the processor until you get a fine meal.

Alternatively, a dry grinder will work. Grind the almonds and flour together, making sure you do it in short pulses. Then whisk in the sugar and baking soda.

Transfer to a large bowl and whisk in the oats. Reserve.

Heat the clarified butter/ghee and whisk in the salted caramel sauce until smooth.

Fold the reserved dry mix into the wet mix until just combined. The dough will be a little stiff.

Transfer immediately to the prepared tin and spread evenly using an offset spatula.

Bake for approximately 20–25 minutes until golden brown and firm to the touch.

Leave to cool for 5 minutes, then top with Nutella, spreading uniformly.

Scatter the top with slivered almonds. Allow to cool completely, then refrigerate for a couple of hours, or overnight.

Cut into squares.

Chocolate & Walnut

OAT TRAYBAKE (EGGLESS)

🍴 MAKES 16 SQUARES

Wholegrain, hearty and indulgent, this is another recipe that came about in response to reader requests. I got several requests for it and I finally nailed it after a couple of attempts.

INGREDIENTS

50 g quinoa flour
50 g all-purpose flour
35 g quick-cooking oats
100 g walnuts, chopped
60 g brown sugar
100 g unsalted butter, chilled, cubed
50 g thick yogurt
100 g dark chocolate chips

TOPPING
200 g dark chocolate, chopped
1 tsp extra virgin olive oil

METHOD

Preheat the oven to 160°C. Line a square 8 x 8 inch baking tin with parchment paper.
Place all ingredients except the chocolate chips in the jar of a food processor. Process in short bursts until it comes together like cookie dough.
Alternatively, use an electric hand-blender.
Fold in the chocolate chips.
Transfer to the prepared tin and spread evenly using an offset spatula.
Bake for approximately 45 minutes, until the top is a light golden brown.
Meanwhile, melt the chocolate in a double boiler or in the microwave. Whisk gently until smooth, then whisk in the extra virgin olive oil.
Cool the bake on the rack for about 10 minutes, then pour the melted chocolate over, gently spreading to corners with an offset spatula.
Don't overwork chocolate as it'll lose its sheen.
Leave to cool completely, then refrigerate for a couple of hours.
Cut into squares.

Bakery-Style Fresh Cherry
COCOA MUFFINS (EGGLESS)

MAKES 8 BAKERY-STYLE MUFFINS OR 12 REGULAR MUFFINS

Last summer, I tried an eggless version of the fresh cherry muffins from my blog with a few changes, and was quite pleased with how nicely they turned out. I think this will work really well with blueberries too. The muffins are simple and so wholesome, a great way to use fruit.

INGREDIENTS

DRY MIX

150 g wholewheat flour
120 g all-purpose flour
2 tsp baking powder
½ tsp baking soda
¼ tsp salt
50 g dark chocolate chips

WET MIX

1 chia egg (1 tbsp chia seeds +
3 tbsp water)
100 g clarified butter/ghee
30 g cocoa powder
220 ml milk
150 g brown sugar
1 tsp vanilla extract
½ cup pitted cherries

TOPPING

Fresh cherries and chocolate
chips

METHOD

Preheat the oven to 180°C. Line a large 8-muffin tray with liners (or a 12-muffin tray for regular-sized muffins).

Whisk together the dry ingredients in a bowl. Reserve.

Mix the chia seeds with the water in a small bowl. Let it stand for 5 minutes until the seeds gel together.
In a large bowl, whisk together the ghee and cocoa powder. Add to it the milk, chia egg, brown sugar and vanilla extract.
Fold the reserved dry mix and pitted fresh cherries into the wet mix until just combined.
Transfer the batter to 8 large muffin liners, or 12 regular ones.
Top with fresh cherries and mini chocolate chips.
Bake at 180°C for about 20 minutes, or until the top is firm to the touch, and a toothpick tester comes out clean.

Dark Chocolate & Fresh Plum
WHOLEWHEAT MERINGUE TRAYBAKE

¶¶ MAKES 16 SQUARES

This traybake always reminds me of our trip to Leh up north in the summer of 2014. Nothing prepared me for that visit. Mountains higher than one can imagine, all made of mud, rocks—actually, huge boulders—and in many places, not a spot of vegetation. The landscape was unreal and took my breath away at times, and left me with 'brown mountains' stamped on my mind.

This traybake was the first thing I made on my return from that trip. It turned out unexpected; rustically beautiful, with unusual tones, the brown sugar meringue peeping out with the dark chocolate melting into it. One bite later, it was pure joy. Moist, chocolatey, with delightful plum undertones, what a fun bake this turned out to be. The plums must have created some berry-like magic in there, the mountainous meringue look, a reminder of that landscape! Such a nostalgic connect.

INGREDIENTS

DRY MIX

75 g wholewheat flour
¾ tsp baking soda
A pinch of salt

CHOCOLATE PLUM MIX

100 g dark chocolate, chopped fine
185 g plum purée (about 4 medium pitted plums, with skin)
2 egg yolks
40 g cocoa powder
1 tsp vanilla extract

METHOD

Preheat the oven to 180°C. Line an 8 x 8 inch square baking tin with parchment paper.

Whisk together the dry ingredients in a bowl. Reserve.

Place the chocolate in a heatproof bowl and melt either in the microwave 30 seconds at a time, or using the double-boiler method. Whisk until smooth and whisk in the plum puree, followed by the egg yolks, one by one. Add the cocoa powder and vanilla extract and whisk until smooth. Reserve.

WET MIX 1

2 egg whites
A pinch of cream of tartar
100 g brown sugar

Beat the egg whites with an electric hand-beater with a pinch of cream of tartar to soft peaks. Add 100 g sugar, 1 tbsp at a time, and continue to beat to stiff peaks. Reserve.

WET MIX 2

100 g unsalted butter, softened
85 g brown sugar

TOPPING

50 g dark chocolate chips

Beat the butter with the 85 g sugar for 2–3 minutes, until smooth. Stir in the dry mix, followed by the chocolate mix, then gently fold in the wet mix 1, reserving about ½ cup of the whipped egg whites for the topping.

Pour the batter into a prepared tin, and level out using an offset spatula. Swirl over the reserved whipped whites, then sprinkle over with chocolate chips.

Bake for approximately an hour or until a toothpick tester comes out with a few moist crumbs. Tent the top with a sheet of aluminium foil if the top is over-browning.

Place on the cooling rack and leave to cool in the tin for about 30 minutes.

Gently turn out of the tin. Slice and serve.

WHAT IF?

If you don't have cream of tartar, you can use ¼ tsp lime juice instead.

Cookies & Biscotti

Simple wholegrain recipes, staple ingredients, usually one-bowl, with fun twists, with egg and without, it's all here! Brownie cookies, oat chocolate chip cookies, chocolate sablés, biscotti, cookie tarts and so on. They are the simplest to turn out, bake up really quick, and so delicious to nibble on. Good to get kids started on baking too!

Dark Chocolate
WHOLEWHEAT & OAT BROOKIES

MAKES 18-24

I began making these several years ago, and they got healthier each time. Every time I said I'd found the cookie I love, along came a new favourite.

This is not your everyday quintessential chocolate chip cookie. This one is better where a deep, dark chocolate brownie meets fudgy cookies. Brownie + Cookies = Brookies!

INGREDIENTS

DRY MIX

75 g wholewheat flour
½ tsp baking soda
80 g quick-cooking oats
A pinch of salt
50 g dark chocolate chips

WET MIX 1

125 g bittersweet chocolate, chopped fine
50 g unsalted butter, softened
30 g cocoa powder

WET MIX 2

1 egg
1 tbsp thick yogurt
100 g brown sugar
½ tsp vanilla extract

METHOD

Preheat the oven to 180°C. Line two cookie trays with parchment paper.

Whisk together the dry ingredients in a small bowl. Reserve.

Place the chocolate and butter from wet mix 1 in a glass bowl and melt using the double-boiler method or in the microwave, 30 seconds at a time.
Whisk until smooth, then stir in the cocoa powder. Reserve.

Place the egg, yogurt, brown sugar and vanilla extract of wet mix 2 in a large bowl. Using an electric hand-mixer, beat until fluffy.
Stir in wet mix 1 until well incorporated, then stir in the reserved dry mix with the chocolate chips.
Let the dough sit for 5 minutes for the oats to absorb moisture. If the dough looks a little 'wet', then add in an extra spoonful of oats.
Take walnut-sized bits, or use a cookie scoop to measure a portion. Using your palms, bring the dough together to form a ball. Flatten slightly and place on the cookie tray. Flatten gently with the base of a glass or using a fork.
For a fudgy cookie, bake for 15–20 minutes or until the tops feel firm. For firmer cookies, bake for a further 5 minutes.
Leave to cool for 5 minutes on the tray, then cool completely on a cooling rack.
If the weather is warm, store these in an airtight container and refrigerate.

(**Note:** *Cookies firm up after being baked so don't be tempted to over-bake them. You might end up with dry cookies.*)

Addictive Fudgy
BROOKIES (EGGLESS)

MAKES 20-24

I've made several versions of these eggless cookies over time and loved each one. I find this version particularly addictive, the coconut sugar and coffee powder adding deep flavour. I'll probably never need another eggless brownie cookie recipe!

INGREDIENTS

DRY MIX

100 g wholewheat flour
¼ tsp baking soda
½ tsp baking powder
¼ tsp salt
50 g dark chocolate chips

WET MIX

1 chia egg (1 tbsp chia seeds + 3 tbsp water)
115 g unsalted butter, softened
50 g brown sugar
50 g coconut sugar
½ tsp vanilla extract
1 tbsp instant coffee powder
30 g cocoa powder

TOPPING

Mini morsels/chocolate chips (optional)

METHOD

Whisk together the dry ingredients in a small bowl. Reserve.

In a small bowl, stir together the water and chia seeds. Leave to stand for 5 minutes to gel while you mix the other ingredients.

In the bowl of a stand mixer, beat together the butter and both sugars. Alternatively, use a large bowl and an electric hand-mixer.

Beat in the chia egg and vanilla extract, followed by the coffee powder and cocoa powder.

Lastly, on low speed, fold in the reserved dry mix until just mixed. Don't over-mix.

Now begin preheating the oven while you scoop out the dough! Preheat the oven to 180°C. Line two cookie trays with parchment paper.

Take walnut-sized bits, or use a cookie scoop to measure the portions and bring the dough together to form a ball. Place on the cookie tray and flatten gently with the base of a glass or using a fork. Sprinkle mini chocolate chips, if using.

Bake for 13–15 minutes until firm to the touch.

Leave to cool for 5 minutes on the tray, then cool completely on a cooling rack.

The cookies will continue to firm up as they cool. These are fudgy and soft in the centre, very moist too. If you'd like firmer cookies, possibly reduce the temperature to 170°C and bake them for 5–7 minutes longer. Do keep a close eye on them towards the end, though, as dark chocolate cookies can go from done to burnt in next to no time!

Chocolate & Nutella

WHOLEGRAIN COOKIES

MAKES 24

Healthy, wholegrain, deep, dark, soft, cakey chocolate cookies, with a Nutella heart.

INGREDIENTS

DRY MIX

130 g wholewheat flour
85 g quick-cooking oats
40 g almond meal
½ tsp baking powder
½ tsp salt
¼ tsp baking soda
200 g brown sugar
40 g cocoa powder

WET MIX

100 g unsalted butter, softened
2 eggs
¾ tsp vanilla extract

FILLING

50 g Nutella

METHOD

Add all the ingredients of the dry mix to the bowl of a stand mixer and mix at low speed.
Alternatively, use a large bowl and an electric hand-mixer.

In a small bowl, whisk together the wet mix and add it to the dry mix. Mix briefly at low speed until the cookie dough comes together. It should hold when pinched between the fingertips.
Divide the dough into 24 balls and refrigerate for half an hour.
Line two cookie trays with parchment paper.
Flatten each into a disk, then place ½ tsp of Nutella in the centre and pull up the dough around it. Gently roll back into a ball and flatten slightly. Place on the prepared tray. Repeat with rest.

Place the trays in the freezer while you preheat the oven to 180°C.
Bake for approximately 20–25 minutes until the cookies feel firm to the touch.
Leave to cool for 5 minutes on the tray, then cool completely on a cooling rack.
These are best consumed within 2–3 days.

Instead of flattening and filling the disks, you could even make thumbprint cookies!
Make slightly smaller balls and indent the balls with your thumb and add a teaspoon of Nutella. Bake for 15–18 minutes, until light golden brown and firm to the touch.

Chocolate & Walnut
BUCKWHEAT GROATS BISCOTTI

MAKES 30

Chocolatey and so satisfying, the Buckwheat Groats Biscotti is healthy and delicious.

Talking about wholegrains and baking at a TEDx event at Delhi University several years ago, the students happily engaged with my non-stop rambling about food, looking at ingredients differently, and making them count. I mentioned that I had baked buckwheat cookies the previous day and had some in my bag if anyone wished to try some.

Imagine my surprise to find a long queue of young men and women patiently waiting for a taste when I exited the auditorium after the talk! I instantly wished I had baked a double batch.

This biscotti remains my connect to that winter morning and the queue in the corridors of the college!

INGREDIENTS

DRY MIX

150 g wholewheat flour
50 g quick-cooking oats
1½ tsp baking powder
A pinch of salt

WET MIX

75 g dark chocolate, melted
50 g unsalted butter, softened
60 g buckwheat groats, soaked overnight, drained well
75 g brown sugar
1 egg
1 tsp vanilla extract
15 g thick yogurt, if required
50 g chocolate chips
50 g walnuts, chopped

TOPPING

1–2 tbsp brown sugar

METHOD

Preheat the oven to 180°C. Line two cookie trays with parchment paper.

Whisk together the dry ingredients in a small bowl. Reserve.

In the bowl of a stand mixer, whisk all the ingredients for the wet mix together.
Alternatively, use a large bowl and an electric hand-mixer.
Add the reserved dry mix to the wet mix. Mix at low speed until it all comes together. Add the yogurt **only** if required to bring the dough together. Biscotti dough is meant to be quite firm.
Stir in the chocolate chips and walnuts.
Bring the dough together with your hands.
Divide into two and shape into firm logs, about 10 inches long.
Transfer to the prepared tray. Slightly wet your hands and moisten the outside of the roll, and sprinkle over with brown sugar, pressing the sugar gently into place.
Bake for about 20 minutes until the logs are firm to the touch.
Remove from the oven and reduce the oven temperature to 160°C.
Using a sharp, serrated knife, slice the logs thinly, about ½ inch slices, and lay flat on the cookie tray, cut side up.
Return to the oven and bake for approximately 25–30 minutes until firm.
Leave to cool for 5 minutes on the tray, then cool completely on a cooling rack.

Salted Butter & Chocolate Chunk
WHOLEGRAIN SHORTBREAD COOKIES (EGGLESS)

MAKES 12

Buttery, crisp and delicious, this Salted Butter and Chocolate Chunk Wholegrain Shortbread cookie is adapted from a recipe by Alison Roman that took Instagram by storm in February 2018. These cookies offer you everything and more you might want in a cookie. My version is egg-free and partly wholegrain.

INGREDIENTS

125 g salted butter, softened
25 g sugar
50 g brown sugar
1 tsp vanilla extract
75 g all-purpose flour
75 g wholewheat flour
½ tsp baking powder
100 g bittersweet chocolate, chopped into chunks

TOPPING
1–2 tbsp vanilla sugar, for rolling
Flaky sea salt

METHOD

In the bowl of a stand mixer, add all the ingredients, except the chocolate, and mix until they come together to form a cookie dough. Alternatively, use a large bowl and an electric hand-mixer.

At the lowest speed, stir in the chocolate chunks.

Bring together, then roll into a log about 2–2¼ inches in diameter. Wrap tightly in clingwrap and smoothen the logs, pushing together firmly.

Refrigerate for about 2 hours, until firm enough to slice without losing shape.

Preheat the oven to 170°C. Line a cookie tray with parchment paper. Wet your hands slightly and moisten the outside of the roll. Roll in vanilla sugar.

Slice the log into 12–13 half-inch-thick rounds. Lay on the baking sheet, and sprinkle with sea salt.

Bake for about 18–20 minutes until golden at the edges and firm. Leave to cool for 5 minutes on the tray, then cool completely on a cooling rack.

Chocolate & Buckwheat
WHOLEGRAIN SABLÉS (EGGLESS)

MAKES 15–18

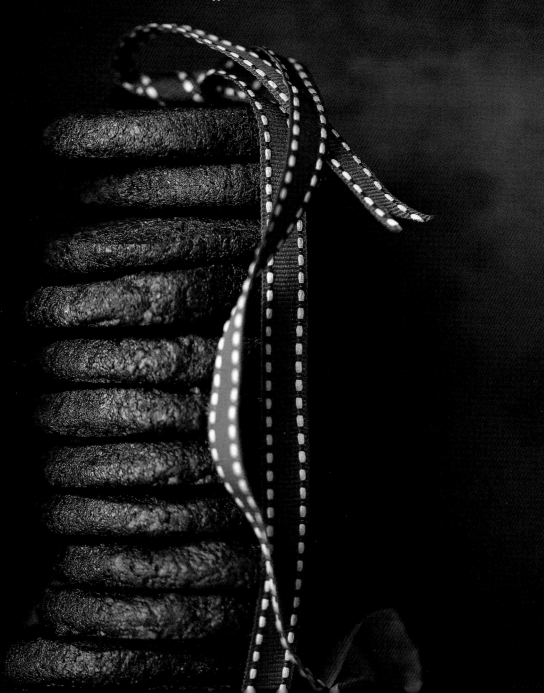

*I didn't expect things to go quite this well when I experimented with wholewheat and buckwheat in this buttery chocolate shortbread. The flavours are deep, and the shortbread crisp and buttery like it should be. Inspired by Salted Black Cocoa Sablés by Ed Kimber @**theboywhobakes**, these are one of my best chocolate shortbread cookies to date.*

Great for the holiday cookie platter, good to hang on the Christmas tree, this shortbread also makes for a nice edible gift!

INGREDIENTS

DRY MIX

50 g wholewheat flour
50 g buckwheat flour
50 g all-purpose flour
125 g dark chocolate, ground
(or chopped fine)
½ tsp baking soda
¼ tsp sea salt

WET MIX

100 g unsalted butter, softened
100 g brown sugar
1 tsp vanilla extract

METHOD

Stir together the dry ingredients in a bowl to mix. Reserve.

In the bowl of a stand mixer, add the butter, brown sugar and vanilla and whisk on a medium speed for 3–4 minutes until smooth and fluffy. Alternatively, use a large bowl and an electric hand-mixer.
Stir in the reserved dry mix by hand to bring the dough together. Don't over-mix, else the cookies will become hard.
Roll the dough into an 8" X 2" log, clingwrap and refrigerate for a few hours until firm. Using a sharp, serrated knife, slice the logs thinly, into about ½ inch slices.
Alternatively, you could bring the dough together into a ball, flatten and clingwrap, then refrigerate as above. Roll out the dough and stamp out cookies with a cookie cutter.
Preheat the oven to 170°C. Line two cookie trays with parchment paper.
Place the cookies on the prepared tray about 2 inches apart. Place the trays in the freezer while the oven preheats. Bake for 12–15 minutes until just firm to the touch.
Leave to cool for 5 minutes on the tray, then cool completely on a cooling rack.

*(**Note:** I often run the dry mix ingredients with roughly chopped chocolate in a hand blender. This also helps mix all the ingredients together well. Sorghum flour/jowar ka atta instead of buckwheat flour works equally well in these cookies.)*

Chocolate & Walnut

WHOLEGRAIN BISCOTTI (EGGLESS)

⚔ MAKES 10-12

When I began baking at home several moons ago, biscotti was very popular at local coffee shops. At the time, my biscotti was almost 'tooth-breakingly' good and very low on fat. The twice-baked Italian cookie always took me back to a vacation in Italy in the 1990s, where an espresso with biscotti was what dreams were made of.

This recipe changed everything. My son took one bite of the updated eggless version and said, 'I began to hate biscotti because it was always so hard and difficult to eat. This is really good!' Just goes to prove that simple ingredients if used right can quite easily please cookie monsters!

INGREDIENTS

DRY MIX

85 g wholewheat flour
30 g all-purpose flour
A pinch of salt

WET MIX

1 chia egg (1 tbsp chia seeds +
3 tbsp water)
40 g clarified butter/ghee,
melted
60 g brown sugar
1 tsp instant coffee powder
15 g cocoa powder
1 tsp vanilla extract
25 g walnuts, chopped
40 g dark chocolate chips

METHOD

Preheat the oven to 180°C. Line a cookie tray with parchment paper.

Whisk together the dry ingredients in a small bowl. Reserve.

In a small bowl, stir together the water and chia seeds. Leave to stand for 5 minutes to gel while you mix the other ingredients.
In a large bowl, whisk together the wet mix ingredients with the chia egg until combined well.
Stir in the dry mix. Bring together to form a smooth log, about 10–12 inches long, patting firmly into shape.
Gently touch with barely moist hands, and sprinkle over with brown sugar.
Bake at 180°C for 20 minutes.
Remove the tray from the oven and leave the biscotti log on the tray for 20 minutes.
Reduce the oven temperature to 170°C.
Now slice diagonally with a sharp knife. Be gentle but firm.
Lay the sliced biscotti sideways on the tray and bake again for a further 20 minutes.
Leave to cool for 5 minutes on the tray, then cool completely on a cooling rack.

Bakery-Style Stovetop
COOKIE-FOR-ONE (EGGLESS)

🍴 MAKES 1 LARGE

The pandemic gave me loads of time to experiment. I'm also grateful for the several requests for no-oven bakes that set the ball in motion. There's something eternally charming about HUGE bakery-style cookies, the sort you see in quaint cafés, that magic of 'ONE BIG COOKIE ONLY FOR ME!'

This cookie is delicious and also wholegrain, so guilt-free in my opinion. If you're craving that bake or slice of cake with coffee, this cookie might hit the spot. I really enjoyed making this on the stovetop. The only difficult thing is waiting for it to cool completely.

INGREDIENTS

WET MIX

1 chia egg (1 tbsp chia seeds + 3 tbsp water)
2 tbsp clarified butter/ghee

DRY MIX

3 tbsp wholewheat flour
1 tbsp quick-cooking oats
2 tbsp brown sugar
1 tbsp cocoa powder
¼ tsp instant coffee powder
¼ tsp baking powder
⅛ tsp baking soda
A pinch of salt
1–2 tbsp dark chocolate chips

METHOD

Preheat the oven to 180°C. Line a cookie tray with parchment paper.

Whisk together the dry ingredients in a small bowl. Reserve.

In a large bowl, stir together the water and chia seeds. Leave to stand for 5 minutes to gel, then whisk in the clarified butter/ghee.
Add the reserved dry mix to the wet mix using the fingertips, and bring together to form a cookie dough.
Place the dough on the prepared tray and pat into a flat, round cookie shape, about 3–4 inches in diameter. (You could use a 4 inch dessert ring and push the dough into shape to get a neat circle.)
Top with a few chocolate chips if desired. The dough doesn't spread much while baking.
Bake in the oven for 10–15 minutes, until firm to the touch. Allow it to cool completely on the tray as it is fragile when warm.

(**Note:** *This can be baked on the stovetop in a preheated, lidded, cast-iron pan on parchment paper placed on a trivet.*)

Two-Minute Microwave
WHOLEGRAIN CHOCOLATE CHIP COOKIES (EGGLESS)

♨ MAKES 4

That these are 100% wholegrain, eggless and baked in the microwave makes the charm of quick, freshly baked, home-made cookies even more rewarding. Credit for these go to the daughter who took my cookie-for-one stovetop recipe and baked them quite easily in the microwave. Not a very keen microwave bake until then, I wasted no time and began experimenting almost immediately!

INGREDIENTS

DRY MIX

3 tbsp wholewheat flour
3 tbsp quick-cooking oats
1 tbsp brown sugar
1 tbsp vanilla sugar (or plain)
¼ tsp baking powder
⅛ tsp baking soda
A pinch of salt
1–2 tbsp dark chocolate chips

WET MIX

2½ tbsp clarified butter/ghee, melted, cooled
1 chia egg (1 tbsp chia seeds + 3 tbsp water)
1 tbsp toasted almonds/ walnuts/pistachios, chopped roughly

METHOD

Whisk together the dry ingredients in a small bowl. Reserve.

In a large bowl, stir together the water and chia seeds. Leave to stand for 5 minutes to gel, then whisk in the clarified butter/ghee.
Add the reserved dry mix to the wet mix using the fingertips, and bring together to form a cookie dough.
Divide into four, shape into firm balls, press down with the fingertips, then flatten with the base of a glass.
Bake on a sheet of parchment paper for 1½ minutes on full power.
Check if firm, else bake for a further 30 seconds. Repeat if required.
Cool completely on a cooling rack.

WHAT IF?

If you want to personalize the flavour, you can experiment with cinnamon powder, coffee, orange zest, etc. Frozen berries will also be lovely!

Malted Chocolate

WHOLEGRAIN COOKIES (EGGLESS)

MAKES 12–15

During the pandemic, when almost the entire world was in some sort of lockdown, the movement of goods was limited. Most shops, both online and offline, ran out of things like cocoa powder and baking chocolate. It was time to improvise with whatever was available. Thankfully, things like drinking chocolate and Bournvita were still available, so malted cookies showed up!

INGREDIENTS

WET MIX

75 g clarified butter/ghee, room temperature
1 chia egg (1 tbsp chia seeds + 3 tbsp water)

DRY MIX

75 g Bournvita
100 g wholewheat flour
50 g quick-cooking oats
½ tsp baking powder
¼ tsp baking soda
A pinch of salt

METHOD

Preheat the oven to 170°C. Line a cookie tray with parchment paper.

In a bowl, stir together the water and chia seeds. Leave to stand for 5 minutes to gel, then whisk in the clarified butter/ghee. Reserve.

In the bowl of a stand mixer, stir together the dry mix ingredients. Alternatively, use a large bowl and an electric hand-mixer.
Add the wet mix to the dry mix. Stir together at low speed. The mixture should come together when pinched between your fingertips. Take walnut-sized bits, or use a cookie scoop to measure a portion and bring the dough together to form a ball. Place on the cookie tray and flatten gently with the base of a glass or using a fork.
Bake for 18–20 minutes or till the cookies are a light golden brown. The cookies may feel soft as they come out of the oven, but they firm up as they cool.
Leave to cool for 5 minutes on the tray, then cool completely on a cooling rack.

*(**Note:** These cookies are slightly on the less sweeter side, but get addictive one bite down. You could add 50g sugar to the dry mix if you like sweeter cookies.)*

Quinoa Chocolate Chip
COOKIES (EGGLESS, GLUTEN-FREE)

MAKES 18-24

These cookies came about because I had some leftover cooked quinoa in the fridge while experimenting with recipes. Deeply chocolatey, crisp, buttery and satisfying, these cookies are quick to make, or rather, super-quick and super-easy.

Do also try the quinoa brownies that use cooked quinoa (page 83).

INGREDIENTS

50 g unsalted butter, softened
100 g jaggery powder
100 g cooked quinoa, cooled
50 g quick-cooking oats
100 g dark chocolate, chopped fine
30 g cocoa powder
1 tsp baking powder
A pinch of salt

METHOD

Preheat the oven to 160°C. Line two cookie trays with parchment paper.

Place all ingredients in the bowl of a food processor and process on high speed until well mixed and the mixture comes together as cookie dough.

Take walnut-sized bits, or use a cookie scoop to measure out a portion. Using your palms, bring the dough together to form a ball. Place on the cookie tray. Flatten gently with the base of a glass or using a fork. Sprinkle over with cooked quinoa if you like.

Bake on the prepared tray for approximately 20–25 minutes, or until firm to the touch.

Turn off the oven and leave inside for 10 minutes.

Leave to cool for 5 minutes on the tray, then cool completely on a cooling rack.

*(**Note:** You will need a food processor for this recipe.)*

Buckwheat Oats Chocolate Chip
COOKIES & A 'TARTOOKIE'
(EGGLESS)

The lockdown gave me a chance to revisit my favourite recipes from the blog. This recipe is from 2014—the original was made with amaranth flour and ginger and is as good. I made a small tart too to check if the dough would work for a tart. It worked like magic, so I've shared the 'tartookie' (tart+cookie) recipe as well.

Wholegrain, nutty, eggless and quite satisfying, here's yet another fuss-free recipe using simple ingredients.

INGREDIENTS

100 g + 50 g quick-cooking oats
50 g buckwheat flour
50 g walnuts
100 g unsalted butter, chilled, cubed
50 g brown sugar
A pinch of salt
1 chia egg (1 tbsp chia seeds + 3 tbsp water)
½ tsp baking soda
30 g honey
80 g dark chocolate chips

METHOD

Preheat the oven to 170°C. Line a cookie tray with parchment paper. In a small bowl, stir together the water and chia seeds. Leave to stand for 5 minutes to gel while you mix the other ingredients.

Place 100 g oats, buckwheat flour, walnuts, butter, sugar and salt in the bowl of a food processor and blend to a fine meal.

Alternatively, a dry grinder will work. Grind the 100 g oats, walnuts and buckwheat flour together, making sure you do it in short pulses. Then cut in the butter with a fork or your fingertips and stir in the salt and sugar.

Add the chia egg, baking soda, remaining oats and the honey. Stir at a low speed to mix, then fold in the chocolate chips.

Take walnut-sized bits or use a cookie scoop to measure out a portion and bring the dough together to form a ball. Place on the cookie tray and flatten gently with the base of a glass or using a fork. Sprinkle over with oats and chocolate chips, or brown sugar.

Bake for about 20 minutes until light golden brown and firm to the touch. Leave to cool for 5 minutes on the tray, then cool completely on a cooling rack.

Optional: Buckwheat Oat Walnut Chocolate Tart or 'Tartookie'
The cookie dough works really well as a tart base as well!

For the tart, make 15 cookies and press the remaining dough into a 4 inch loose-bottomed tart tin firmly, building the sides first, then the base.

Bake for about 15–20 minutes until golden brown and fragrant.
Cool completely in the tin, then loosen the sides gently.

FILLING

100 g bittersweet chocolate,
chopped fine
200 ml cream

Place the chocolate in a glass bowl.
Heat the cream till hot but not boiling and pour over the chocolate.
Allow to stand for 10–15 minutes until the chocolate softens, then stir
gently until smooth. Repeat twice after every 20 minutes, then pour
the filling into the cooled tart base.
Level with an offset spatula and refrigerate for a couple of hours, until
set.

TOPPING

Fresh berries, seasonal fruit,
candied nuts, etc.

Top with berries, seasonal fruit, candied nuts, etc.

Special Occasion Cakes

Chocolate makes every occasion special, so something exceptional is always nice, a cake that screams decadence. Make that something special for the chocolate lover in your life. These cakes might look like you worked on them all day, yet most of the recipes are simple, the steps are broken down, and are often make-ahead. With tips to garnish and present them, I've got you covered. All you need to do is whip out the camera, take a picture, then serve it!

Dark Chocolate
MOUSSE CAKE

MAKES ONE 8 INCH CAKE

Chocolatey, chocolatey, chocolatey, this Dark Chocolate Mousse Cake is a chocolate lover's delight. A really nice cake for a special occasion. The instructions might appear a little involved, but once you read them a couple of times, you'll find it's not too difficult. After all, a special-occasion cake must have 'some work' to make it special!

The Savoiardi or ladyfinger biscuit cake base is from when I joined a worldwide group of Daring Bakers in 2008, and we baked for a challenge every month, only to reveal it to each other on one specific date. The 27th of every month was the highlight of our lives, where we used to race to discover each other's take on the challenge. I learnt much of what I know from then!

INGREDIENTS

SAVOIARDI BISCUIT CAKE BASE

DRY MIX

65 g all-purpose flour
25 g cocoa powder

WET MIX 1

4 egg whites
45 g brown sugar, divided

WET MIX 2

4 egg yolks
45 g brown sugar
1 vanilla bean, scraped
20 g icing sugar, for sifting

METHOD

Preheat the oven to 200°C. Draw out three 7 inch circles on parchment paper.

Sift the flour and cocoa powder twice. Reserve.

In a clean, grease-free bowl, beat the egg whites until soft peaks form. Gradually, add half the brown sugar, and continue beating until the egg whites form firm peaks, glossy and smooth. Reserve.

In another large bowl, combine the egg yolks, remaining brown sugar and scraped vanilla bean. Whip until pale in colour and thick, 3–4 minutes.

With a silicon spatula, gently fold about a third of the whipped whites into the yolks to lighten them up.

Then spoon half of the remaining whites over the yolk mixture. Sift half of the dry mix over the same. Gently fold until the ingredients are barely combined. Repeat with the two remaining halves of the whipped whites and dry mix, folding gently until combined. (It is important to fold very gently and not overdo the folding. Otherwise the batter will deflate and lose volume, resulting in a flat ladyfinger base rather than a spongy one.)

Fit a pastry bag with a plain tip about ½ inch wide first and fill with the batter. Pipe the batter to fill up the three 7 inch circles.

Sift half the icing sugar over the Savoiardi biscuit base and wait for 5 minutes, then sift the remaining sugar. This helps to give the Savoiardi biscuit base its characteristic crispness.

Bake each biscuit base for 12–15 minutes until puffy and firm to the touch.

Cool for 5 minutes on a cooling rack, and then gently turn over and peel off the parchment. Immediately trim, if required, into 7 inch circles using the dessert ring as your guide. Cool completely.

(**Note:** *This can be made a day before.*)

SIMPLE SYRUP

50 g brown sugar
60 ml water
½ tsp vanilla extract

Place all ingredients in a small saucepan and simmer gently until the sugar dissolves. Take off the heat and leave to cool.

DARK CHOCOLATE MOUSSE

250 g dark chocolate
1 tbsp instant coffee powder
400 ml cream
1 tbsp gelatine sprinkled over
25 ml water
100 g brown sugar

Sprinkle the gelatine over the water in a small bowl and leave until spongy. Place the bowl in warm water and leave until the gelatine is clear.

Place the chocolate in a glass bowl. Heat 100 ml cream till hot but not boiling and pour over the chocolate. Allow to stand for 10–15 minutes until the chocolate softens. Stir gently until smooth, then whisk in the coffee powder and gelatine. Leave the chocolate to come to room temperature, stirring on and off.

Meanwhile, whip the remaining 300 ml cream with the brown sugar to medium-stiff peaks. Fold 2 tbsp of the whipped cream through the chocolate mixture to loosen it a bit. Fold half in very gently, then the remaining.

DARK CHOCOLATE FROSTING

200 g bittersweet chocolate, chopped fine
300 ml cream

Place the chocolate in a glass bowl. Heat the cream till hot but not boiling and pour over the chocolate. Allow to stand for 10–15 minutes until the chocolate softens, then stir gently until smooth. Repeat twice after every 20 minutes. Cool until it reaches a spreadable consistency.

100 g dark chocolate for shards

To make the shards, melt the chocolate in the microwave. Stir until smooth. With an offset spatula (or butter knife), thinly spread the melted chocolate on to one strip of 3 x 12 inch parchment paper. Place another strip of parchment paper on top and roll tightly into a scroll. Secure and put in the freezer for about 15 minutes (or until required). Unroll over a platter and use on top of the cake.

(**Note:** *Can be made ahead and stored in an airtight box in the fridge.*)

ASSEMBLE

Place a biscuit disc within an adjustable dessert ring on a cake platter. Brush liberally with syrup and top with one-third of the chocolate mousse filling. Repeat with remaining discs, finishing with a mousse layer on top.
Cover and refrigerate overnight.
Gently remove the dessert ring. Use a warm towel wrapped around the outside to help release it, if required. Frost with the dark chocolate frosting, and wrap the lace collar around the sides. Top with dark chocolate shards.
Leave out of the fridge for 30 minutes before serving.

LACE COLLAR

100 g dark chocolate, melted

Stir the melted chocolate until smooth and put into a disposable piping bag.
To make a lace collar for the cake, measure the height of the border that you would like, and the circumference of the cake. Cut out the parchment paper to this measure, snip off a tiny hole on the piping bag and squiggle patterns or doodle with the melted chocolate.
Wait for it to almost set, about 5 minutes in the fridge in summer, where the paper is still flexible and the chocolate is not set hard. Wrap it around the cake and press gently to the frosted sides so that the pattern sticks to the sides.
Return to the fridge to set, about 30 minutes.
Gently peel off the parchment paper.

Dark Chocolate & Coffee
ROULADE

MAKES ONE 12 INCH ROULADE

If you asked me what pairs best with chocolate, my answer would be coffee. I often dream of coffee-based desserts, and one example is this quick Dark Chocolate and Coffee Roulade that comes together with minimal fuss. If you love coffee too, then this cake is for you. Paired with a dark chocolate ganache, flavoured with a hint of Kahlúa, dressed up with doodles, what's not to love about this Swiss roll.

A touch as simple as piping a design over it with melted chocolate lifts it to something extraordinary, inspired by henna/mehndi on hands at Indian weddings.

INGREDIENTS

COFFEE ROULADE

3 eggs
100 g brown sugar
55 g all-purpose flour
1 tbsp instant coffee powder
1 tsp vanilla extract
1 tbsp icing sugar

COFFEE SYRUP

60 ml water
25 g brown sugar
1 tsp instant coffee powder
1 tsp Kahlúa (optional)

METHOD

Preheat the oven to 190°C. Line a 15 x 10 inch jelly roll tin with parchment paper.

In a large bowl, using an electric beater, whisk the eggs and brown sugar until tripled in volume and light and mousse-like, about 8 minutes.

Add the coffee and vanilla extract and beat for another minute.

Sift the flour over the whipped eggs, and gently fold in, making sure not to release the beaten air.

Turn the batter into the prepared tin, smoothen out and bake for approximately 25 minutes until light golden and firm to the touch. Keep an eye on it during the last 5 minutes.

Lay a kitchen towel flat on the counter and sift over with powdered sugar. Turn the baked cake on to it, and gently peel off the parchment paper.

Sift over with icing sugar, cover with a sheet of parchment, and roll gently into a tight roll, using the kitchen towel to guide you. Leave to cool completely.

Place all ingredients in a small pan and simmer until the sugar dissolves. Cool and stir in the Kahlúa if using. Reserve.

CHOCOLATE GANACHE FILLING

100 g dark chocolate, chopped fine
150 ml cream
1 tbsp Kahlúa (optional)
Icing sugar, for sifting

Place the chocolate in a glass bowl. Heat the cream till hot but not boiling and pour over the chocolate. Allow to stand for 10–15 minutes until the chocolate softens. Add Kahlúa if using then, stir gently until smooth. Repeat twice after every 20 minutes. Cool completely.

*(**Note**: Reserve 2 tbsp of the ganache in a piping bag if you wish to decorate the outside.)*

ASSEMBLE

Gently unroll the cake, paint over with coffee syrup, and then spread the chocolate ganache all over it. Roll back gently but firmly, wrap in clingwrap and refrigerate with the seam down for an hour or two (or overnight) to allow the flavours to develop.
Unwrap and place on a serving platter. Trim the edges if you like. That gives a neat appearance. Make free-hand designs over the roulade with the reserved ganache placed in a disposable piping bag.

*(**Tip:** Try doodling patterns over a ceramic/steel platter for practice.)*

Bittersweet Chocolate

FALLEN GATEAU

🍴 MAKES ONE 7 INCH CAKE

I've made this fallen cake several times over the years, adapted from an Alice Medrich recipe. This gateau is like an ugly duckling, an almost flourless cake, which gets dressed up to go out. It reminds me of a Shakespearean tragedy as it bakes, the rise followed by the tragic collapse. Left 'undressed', it's a moorish, rustic, sunken cake, beautiful in my eyes. Barely any flour makes it more special, the collar giving it an instant uplift.

INGREDIENTS

GATEAU

100 g bittersweet chocolate, chopped fine
175 g brown sugar (divided 100 g + 75 g)
120 ml freshly brewed hot coffee
50 g cocoa powder
A pinch of sea salt
2 eggs, separated
A pinch of cream of tartar
1 tsp vanilla extract
25 g wholewheat flour
30 g almond meal
15 ml Kirsch
1 tbsp powdered sugar

CRÈME PATISSERIE

100 ml milk
100 ml cream
30 g sugar
1 vanilla bean, split
1 tbsp corn flour

METHOD

Preheat the oven to 190°C. Line a 7 inch springform tin with parchment paper.
Place the egg whites in a clean bowl with the cream of tartar and beat to soft peaks. Add 75 g sugar and continue to beat until stiff peaks form. Reserve.
Place the bittersweet chocolate in a large bowl and soften in the microwave, or using the double-boiler method. Add the remaining 100 g sugar and brewed coffee. Whisk until the chocolate has melted completely.
Add the vanilla extract and egg yolks. Whisk until smooth, then whisk in the cocoa powder.
Now fold in the kirsch, almond meal and flour. Stir gently to mix completely.
Add 2–3 tbsp of the beaten whites to loosen the batter, then add the remaining beaten whites and fold in gently.
Turn the batter into the prepared tin and bake for about 40–45 minutes, until a toothpick tester inserted into the centre comes out moist with a few crumbs hanging.
Cool completely in the tin on a cooling rack.
Gently demould.

Whisk all the ingredients together in a saucepan and bring to a simmering boil, stirring constantly until thickened.
Once the custard has thickened, take it off the heat, discard the vanilla bean shell and strain/pour it into a clean bowl. Cool, cover with clingwrap touching the surface and refrigerate.
(**Note:** *Can be made a day before.*)

LACE COLLAR

100 g dark chocolate, melted

Stir the melted chocolate until smooth and put into a disposable piping bag.

To make a lace collar for the cake, measure the height of the border that you would like, and the circumference of the cake. Cut out the parchment paper to this measure, snip off a tiny hole on the piping bag and squiggle patterns or doodle with the melted chocolate.

Wait for it to almost set, about 5 minutes in the fridge in summer, where the paper is still flexible and the chocolate is not set hard. Wrap it around the cake and press gently to the frosted sides so that the pattern sticks to the sides.

Return to the fridge to set, about 30 minutes.

Gently peel off the parchment paper.

TOPPING

Few sprigs fresh mint
Dark chocolate shavings
200 g balsamic strawberries
(page 259)

Top with crème patisserie and balsamic strawberries, and garnish with sprigs of fresh mint and chocolate shavings.

Dark Chocolate Quinoa
CAKE

MAKES ONE 6 INCH CAKE

This Dark Chocolate Quinoa Cake is a simple, one-bowl cake. Topped with luscious, whipped mascarpone, rose petals and pistachio slivers, this makes a pretty tea or birthday cake.

Flourless and wholegrain cakes have heavier crumbs, and eventually it's a matter of personal taste and habit. This quinoa cake goes back to when I had discovered a love for everything quinoa, a phase you'll find through the book with quinoa-based brownies, cookies and tarts.

INGREDIENTS

QUINOA CAKE

100 g cooked quinoa, chilled
100 g dark chocolate, chopped fine
50 g wholewheat flour
50 g clarified butter/ghee
100 g jaggery powder
1 egg
1 tsp vanilla extract
15 g cocoa powder
1 tsp baking powder
¼ tsp baking soda
1 tbsp thick yogurt

ALMOND CREAM

150 g mascarpone, chilled
2–3 tbsp icing sugar
4–5 drops almond extract
Roasted beet juice to colour the almond cream (optional)

TOPPING

Dried organic rose petals, pistachio slivers

METHOD

Preheat the oven to 160°C. Lightly grease a 6 inch springform tin.

Place the quinoa, dark chocolate and wholewheat flour in the jar of a blender. Process for 10–15 seconds at a time, scraping down each time, until you get a breadcrumb-like mix.
In the bowl of a stand mixer, add this mix to the remaining ingredients for the cake. Stir together at the lowest speed until the batter comes together. Don't over-mix.
Transfer to the prepared tin.
Bake for 35–40 minutes until a toothpick tester comes out clean.
Cool in the tin for 20 minutes, then cool completely on the rack.

Place all the ingredients in a bowl and whisk gently until smooth. Taste and adjust the sweetness if required.

ASSEMBLE

Top with almond cream. Garnish with rose petals and pistachio slivers.
Refrigerate for about an hour before serving.

Chocolate & Strawberry
ROULADE WITH
BURNT HONEY MASCARPONE

🍴 **MAKES ONE 12 INCH ROULADE**

Strawberries pair beautifully with chocolate, a pairing I really enjoy working with. This roulade came about while working with a honey brand, and I love the way it turned out, the burnt honey mascarpone adding special flavour. Once I discovered the charm of burnt honey, that's all I wanted to use. It's a dangerous obsession, but playing with flavours can be quite interesting.

INGREDIENTS

SWISS ROLL

DRY MIX

65 g all-purpose flour
½ tsp baking powder
A pinch of salt

WET MIX

3 egg whites
50 g sugar
½ vanilla bean, scraped
Few drops almond extract
2 egg yolks, whisked lightly

WET MIX 2

1 tbsp oil
2 tbsp milk

METHOD

Preheat the oven to 180°C. Line a 15 x 10 inch jelly roll tin with parchment paper.

Whisk together the dry ingredients in a small bowl. Reserve.

Beat the egg whites, sugar, almond extract and vanilla bean to stiff peaks. Add the whisked yolks and beat briefly at low speed to incorporate.
Sift over the reserved dry mix and fold in gently, making sure not to lose volume.

Whisk together the oil and milk in a small bowl, then whisk in 2 tbsp of the batter.
Now fold this oil and milk mix into the remaining batter.
Spread on to the prepared tin. Tap sharply once to release bubbles. Bake for 20 minutes. Lay a kitchen towel flat on the counter and sift over with powdered sugar. Turn the baked cake on to it, and gently peel off the parchment paper.
Sift over with icing sugar, cover with a sheet of parchment and roll gently into a tight roll, using the kitchen towel to guide you. Leave to cool completely.

HONEY CHOCOLATE GANACHE FILLING

170 g dark chocolate, chopped fine
225 ml cream
1 tbsp honey

Place the chocolate in a glass bowl.
Heat the cream till hot but not boiling and pour over the chocolate.
Allow to stand for 10–15 minutes until the chocolate softens, then add the honey and stir gently until smooth. Repeat twice after every 20 minutes and cool to a spreadable consistency.
Whisk again before use.
Reserve 2–3 tbsp in a piping bag to pipe over the roll.

BURNT HONEY MASCARPONE

225 g mascarpone, chilled
125 g honey
2 tbsp water

Place the honey in a saucepan and simmer until dark amber. Take off the heat, add the water (it will splutter for 30 seconds, so be careful), then stir. Leave to cool completely.
Whisk the mascarpone gently until smooth, then fold in the cooled burnt honey.

FILLING
200 g strawberries, chopped

ASSEMBLE

Gently unroll the cake and spread a layer of the ganache filling over the roll (reserve 1–2 tbsp to pipe over the roulade), followed by a layer of burnt honey mascarpone.
Scatter the chopped strawberries (reserve some for garnishing).
Roll back gently but firmly, wrap in clingwrap and refrigerate with the seam down for an hour or two (or overnight) to allow the flavours to develop.
Unwrap and place on a serving platter. Trim the edges, if you like.
Pipe the reserved ganache filling over the top and sides. Garnish with the reserved strawberries and a sprig of fresh mint.

Chocolate & Coffee Ombré
ZUCCOTTO (EGGLESS)

♨ MAKES ONE 8 INCH TORTE

The Zuccotto is an old favourite that I first had in Milan way back in 1990.
A dessert cake said to be inspired by the cathedral domes of Italy, it's a simple dessert that basically needs a bowl, a whisk and an oven. A bowl to hand-whisk the batter in, then the same bowl to set the dessert in. My version is a coffee and chocolate one, a rather interesting baking project to undertake. A real fun one!

INGREDIENTS

COFFEE SPONGE

60 ml strongly brewed coffee, warm
65 g buttermilk
35 g ghee, melted
1 chia seed egg (1 tbsp chia seeds + 3 tbsp water)
130 g jaggery powder
¼ tsp salt
½ tsp baking powder
½ tsp baking soda
120 g all-purpose flour

FILLING

COFFEE MASCARPONE

200 g mascarpone
1 tbsp instant coffee powder
25 g icing sugar

CHOCOLATE GANACHE FILLING & FROSTING

175 g chocolate, chopped fine
275 ml cream

METHOD

Preheat the oven to 180°C. Line an 8 inch loose-bottomed tin and a 6 inch loose-bottomed tin with parchment paper.

In a large bowl, add the freshly brewed coffee, melted warm ghee, buttermilk, chia seed egg and jaggery powder.
Whisk well until the jaggery powder mixes in. Add the remaining ingredients, salt, baking powder, baking soda and flour, and fold in.
Divide the batter between the tins, 300 g in the 8 inch tin and 150 g in the 6 inch tin.
Bake for 20 minutes.

Whisk all ingredients in a bowl gently until smooth.

Place the chocolate in a large bowl.
Heat the cream and pour over. Stand for 10–15 minutes until the chocolate is soft. Stir until smooth.

ASSEMBLE

Line the same large bowl with clingfilm. Place the larger 8 inch sponge in the bowl, pressing gently into place to form a dome. Add the coffee mascarpone filling, followed by half the chocolate filling. Reserve the rest of the chocolate filling for the frosting. Seal the cake with the 6 inch sponge, pushing it gently into place. Cover with clingwrap, place a small platter with a weight on top to make it compact and leave to set overnight for the flavours to mature. Turn on to a serving platter, remove the clingwrap and frost the cake.

MASCARPONE FROSTING

600 g mascarpone, chilled
75 g icing sugar
1 tbsp instant coffee powder
2 tbsp instant coffee powder

In a bowl, gently whisk the mascarpone and sugar until just smooth. Divide into three portions. Leave one as is, add 1 tbsp coffee powder to the second and mix it in. Add 2 tbsp coffee powder to the third portion. These are the three different shades for the frosting!

Gently heat the reserved ganache over a double boiler to a spreadable consistency.
Spread over the top of the cake using an offset spatula.
Pipe over with the three different-coloured mascarpone for the ombré effect.

Stovetop Chocolate & Coffee
WHOLEWHEAT CAKE (EGGLESS)

MAKES ONE 6 INCH CAKE

Inundated with requests for a no-oven stovetop eggless chocolate cake recipe during the pandemic-induced lockdown, this was what I came up with. My first ever stovetop bake for #quarantinebakers on Instagram turned out rather well and brought me much joy.

Taking hints from how an aunt used to bake years ago, I reworked an earlier recipe and was quite amazed at the result. The cake is 100% wholegrain, with ingredients like clarified butter/ghee, jaggery powder, cocoa powder and a touch of coffee, all easily substitutable. Cocoa powder by itself works just fine, yet I always find that a spoon of coffee added in really enhances the depth of chocolate. You could always add nuts instead of the chocolate chips, or chop up a bar of any chocolate you have on hand, else skip it entirely.

INGREDIENTS

METHOD

Line a 6 inch loose-bottomed tin with parchment paper. Do make sure the tin fits well into the container that you will bake in and ensure that the lid closes.

Put a metal trivet/overturned plate on the base of a heavy-bottomed container with a tight-fitting lid (I used a cast iron Dutch oven). Place on the stovetop over a medium-high heat with the lid in place while you make the batter.

DRY MIX

150 g wholewheat flour
1 tsp baking powder
½ tsp baking soda
A pinch of salt

Whisk together the dry ingredients in a small bowl. Reserve.

WET MIX
100 ml strongly brewed coffee, warm (or 2 tbsp instant coffee powder + hot water)
50 g clarified butter/ghee, melted
150 g condensed milk
35 g jaggery powder
2 tbsp cocoa powder
1 tsp vanilla extract

Add the hot coffee to a large bowl, and whisk in the clarified butter/ghee, condensed milk, jaggery powder, cocoa powder and vanilla extract to mix well. Reserve.

Stir in the reserved dry mix, folding in gently to mix well.

Turn the batter into the prepared tin and tap once to settle the batter.

Carefully take the lid off the hot container, and place the tin inside.

Quickly cover with the fitted lid and reduce the heat to a minimum. Leave untouched for 30 minutes.

Carefully lift the lid and check for doneness with a wooden pick. It

should have a few crumbs sticking, slightly moist. Turn off the heat and leave the tin in for 5–7 minutes, with the lid on.

Remove from the container and cool on the rack for 10–15 minutes at least, then gently demould.

Serve as is, or frost as below.

CHOCOLATE GANACHE

100 g dark chocolate, chopped fine
150 ml cream

Place the chocolate in a glass bowl. Heat the cream till hot but not boiling and pour over the chocolate. Allow to stand for 10–15 minutes until the chocolate softens, then stir gently until smooth. Repeat twice after every 20 minutes. Leave to cool.

Frost the top and sides of the cake with the ganache once it begins to hold form and reaches a spreadable consistency.

Garnish with chocolate shards, non-pareils, berries, etc.

WHAT IF?

If you're using an oven, bake in a preheated oven at 180°C for approximately 25 minutes.

Chocolate & Coffee
LAYERED CAKE (EGGLESS)

MAKES ONE 6 INCH CAKE

Layered cakes are always special, and this is no different. I went eggless with this version and loved how good it tasted. This coffee mascarpone filling is bowl-scrapingly good, as is the whipped dark chocolate ganache. And yes, the lace collar! It has been a favourite way to pretty up cakes, and I've done it for years. I shot a small video specially to show off the lace collar, and how something so simple can add a special touch. Do catch it on my Instagram handle @passionateaboutbaking if you have a moment!

INGREDIENTS

COFFEE CAKE
DRY MIX

200 g all-purpose flour
½ tsp baking soda
1½ tsp baking powder
A pinch of salt

WET MIX

250 g thick yogurt
60 ml neutral oil
50 g clarified butter/ghee, room temperature
150 g light brown sugar
1 tsp coffee extract
1 tbsp coffee powder

FILLING

150 ml cream, chilled
30 g vanilla sugar
1 tbsp instant coffee powder
75 g mascarpone, chilled

METHOD

Preheat oven to 190°C. Line a 6 inch baking tin with parchment paper.

Sift the dry ingredients in a bowl. Reserve.

In a large bowl, whisk the wet ingredients until smooth.
Gradually fold in the reserved dry mix, one-third at a time, until smooth. Don't over-mix.
Transfer to the prepared tin.
Bake initially for 10 minutes at 190°C, then reduce the temperature to 180°C, and bake for another 25–30 minutes, until a toothpick tester comes out with a few moist crumbs.
Cool for 10 minutes, then remove from the tin and cool completely on the cooling rack.
Slice horizontally into three layers. Sandwich the cake layers with the filling, then frost with the ganache. Add a lace collar if desired.

Using an electric hand-beater, whip the cream, sugar and coffee powder on high speed until medium-stiff peaks form. Gently fold in the mascarpone so as to not lose volume.

CHOCOLATE GANACHE

100 g dark chocolate, chopped fine
250 ml cream
15 g honey

Place the chocolate in a glass bowl. Heat the cream till hot but not boiling and pour over the chocolate. Allow to stand for 10–15 minutes until the chocolate softens, then stir gently until smooth. Repeat twice after every 20 minutes. Refrigerate until it is slightly firm, then beat with an electric hand-beater until it's glossy and smooth, and holds peaks. Sandwich the cake layers with the filling, then frost with the ganache.

There's a quick video on my Instagram handle
@passionateaboutbaking

LACE COLLAR

125–150 g dark chocolate, melted

Stir the melted chocolate until smooth and put into a disposable piping bag.
To make a lace collar for the cake, measure the height of the border that you would like, and the circumference of the cake. Cut out parchment paper to this measure, snip off a tiny hole on the piping bag and squiggle patterns or doodle with the melted chocolate.
Wait for it to almost set, with the paper still flexible and the chocolate not set hard. Wrap it around the cake and press gently to the frosted sides so that the pattern sticks to the sides.
Return to the fridge to refrigerate and set, about 30 minutes.
Gently peel off the parchment paper.

Best Dark Chocolate
WHOLEGRAIN CAKE (EGGLESS)

MAKES ONE 6 INCH CAKE

This wholegrain eggless chocolate gateau was the biggest surprise ever! Moist, deep, delicious and with texture like a flourless cake, this cake is vegan sans the frosting. This was the first time I used gram flour or besan while baking with chocolate, and was amazed at the results.

I've topped the cake with a whipped dark chocolate ganache; a coconut cream ganache with non-dairy vegan chocolate will keep the whole gateau vegan. My favourite part of course is the lace chocolate collar which elevates even the most basic of cakes to something really special. Another obsession, though you might have already guessed!

INGREDIENTS

DRY MIX

30 g gram flour (besan)
130 g wholewheat flour
45 g coconut sugar
100 g brown sugar
1 tsp baking soda
¼ tsp salt

WET MIX

200 ml coconut milk
60 ml brewed coffee, hot
45 ml oil
1 tsp vanilla extract
50 g cocoa powder

CHOCOLATE GANACHE FROSTING

150 g dark chocolate, chopped fine
250 ml cream
1 tbsp honey

METHOD

Preheat the oven to 180°C. Line a 6 inch loose-bottomed tin with parchment paper.

Whisk together the dry ingredients in a small bowl. Reserve.

Gently heat the coconut milk, hot coffee and oil in a saucepan on the stovetop or in the microwave in a heatproof bowl. Whisk in the cocoa powder and vanilla extract.
Swiftly mix in the reserved dry mix, then turn the batter into the prepared tin.
Bake for 25–30 minutes, until firm to the touch or a toothpick tester comes out clean.
Cool in the tin for 15 minutes, then gently turn out to cool completely on the rack. Frost as below.

Place the chocolate in a glass bowl. Heat the cream till hot but not boiling and pour over the chocolate. Allow to stand for 10–15 minutes until the chocolate softens, then add the honey and stir gently until smooth. Repeat twice after every 20 minutes. Cool to a spreadable consistency.
Frost the sides and top of the cake.

CHIA VANILLA MACERATED STRAWBERRIES

100 g strawberries, quartered
1 tsp chia seeds
1 tbsp brown sugar
Juice of ½ a small lime

Stir together to mix. Let it stand for about 30 minutes at least to allow the berries to macerate. Strain if they release too much liquid.

LACE COLLAR

100–125 g dark chocolate, melted

Stir the melted chocolate until smooth and put it into a disposable piping bag.

To make a lace collar for the cake, measure the height of the border that you would like, and the circumference of the cake. Cut out parchment paper to this measure, snip off a tiny hole on the piping bag and squiggle patterns or doodle with the melted chocolate.

Wait for it to almost set, where the paper is still flexible and the chocolate is not set hard. Wrap it around the cake and press gently to the frosted sides so that the pattern sticks to the sides.

Return to the fridge to set, about 30 minutes.

Gently peel off the parchment paper.

Add the lace collar and top with the chia vanilla macerated strawberries.

Slice with a knife dipped in hot water.

Cheesecakes

Every home needs a cheesecake to show up at least once in a while so that everyone can enjoy this classic, indulgent dessert. I am sharing several different types that I have made over the years; some baked, some not, some with egg, others egg-free. In my opinion, cheesecakes hold an eternal charm and are real crowd-pleasers.

At the risk of repeating myself, it's worth adding that *quality ingredients are key!*

Foolproof Dark Chocolate
CHEESECAKE

MAKES ONE 8 INCH CHEESECAKE

Dark, divine, sinful, creamy, chocolatey and, above all, as simple as can be, this Foolproof Dark Chocolate Cheesecake will leave you wanting more. We all need that one cheesecake recipe that we can literally shut our eyes and throw together. This is one of them. Very simple and quite fuss-free, the recipe is adapted from one that my friend Ruchira makes often.

INGREDIENTS

BISCUIT BASE

150 g digestive biscuits
20 g brown sugar
30 g cocoa powder
50 g unsalted butter, melted, cooled

DARK CHOCOLATE FILLING

3 eggs
200 g dark chocolate, melted
400 g cream cheese, room temperature
200 ml cream
150 g brown sugar
35 g cocoa powder
1 tsp vanilla extract

GANACHE

75 g dark chocolate, chopped fine
100 ml cream

METHOD

Run the biscuits, brown sugar and cocoa powder in a blender to fine crumbs.
Alternatively place the biscuits in a Ziploc bag and crush to make fine crumbs.
Stir in the sugar and cocoa powder, then stir in the melted butter.
Push into the base and work up the sides of the tart tin.
Press into an 8 inch loose-bottomed tin and place in the freezer while you make the filling.

Preheat the oven to 160°C.

Place all the ingredients for the filling in the bowl of a food processor, and blend well to mix, for 1–2 minutes on medium speed.
Alternatively, use a large bowl and an electric hand-mixer.
Pour the filling into the chilled crust.
Bake for one hour until the filling is firm to the touch.
Cool completely in the oven, then cover and refrigerate overnight.
Top as below.

Place the chocolate in a glass bowl. Heat the cream till hot but not boiling and pour over the chocolate. Allow to stand for 10–15 minutes until the chocolate softens, then stir gently until smooth. Repeat twice after every 20 minutes. Refrigerate until it is slightly firm, then beat with an electric hand-beater until glossy and smooth, and holds peaks. Spread over the chilled cheesecake.

Chocolate & Macerated Berries
CHEESECAKE

🍴 MAKES ONE 8 INCH CHEESECAKE

One of my favourite ways to serve dessert is to include the goodness of fresh fruit that is in season, especially strawberries and cherries. I think fruit uplifts dessert, giving it refreshing notes, and also adding the drama of colour!

This recipe is a variation on the Foolproof Dark Chocolate Cheesecake. Since one NEEDS a cheesecake every so often, I go about tweaking the recipe here and there depending on what I have on hand. Minimal fuss, maximum taste, this takes under 20 minutes to come together.

INGREDIENTS

BISCUIT BASE

100 g digestive biscuits
50 g whole almonds
30 g cocoa powder
20 g jaggery powder
70 g clarified butter/ghee ,
melted, cooled

FILLING

3 eggs
200 g dark chocolate, melted
300 g cream cheese, room
temperature
200 ml cream
90 g jaggery powder
30 g cocoa powder
1 tsp vanilla extract

GANACHE

75 g dark chocolate, chopped
fine
100 ml cream

RED WINE MACERATED BERRIES

250 g strawberries, chopped
50–75 g brown sugar
2–3 star anise
Zest of **1** orange
100 ml red wine
40 ml orange juice

METHOD

Place digestive biscuits, almonds, cocoa powder and jaggery powder
in the processor. Blend to a fine meal.
Alternatively, a dry grinder will work. Work in short pulses.
Stir in the melted clarified butter/ghee.
Press into an 8 inch loose-bottomed tin and place in the freezer while
you make the filling.

Preheat the oven to 160°C.

Place all the ingredients for the filling in the bowl of a food processor,
and blend well to mix, for 1–2 minutes on medium speed.
Alternatively, use a large bowl and an electric hand-mixer.
Pour the filling into the crust.
Bake for one hour until the filling is firm to the touch.
Cool completely in the oven, then cover and refrigerate overnight.
Top as below.

Place the chocolate in a glass bowl. Heat the cream till hot but not
boiling and pour over the chocolate. Allow to stand for 10–15 minutes
until the chocolate softens, then stir gently until smooth. Repeat twice
after every 20 minutes. Refrigerate until it is slightly firm, then beat
with an electric hand-beater until glossy and smooth, and holds peaks.

In a non-reactive bowl, put in the strawberries, star anise, orange zest
and brown sugar. Stir to mix, then pour in the wine. Stand covered in
the fridge overnight.
Discard the star anise and strain the strawberries. Reserve in a bowl.
Place strained wine in a small saucepan with the orange juice, and
simmer until thick and syrupy. Taste and adjust the sweetness if
required. Cool slightly, then pour over the strawberries, and refrigerate
until required. The strawberries can be made a day ahead if desired.
Ladle the strawberries over the ganache. If the syrup is thin, reduce it
further until nice and thick. Cool and pour over strawberries.
(**Note:** *Can be made 2–3 days ahead of time.*)

For a non-alcoholic version: If you wish to skip the red wine, use
1–2 tbsp of balsamic vinegar instead. Taste and adjust the sweetness,
adding just 50 g to begin with.

Baked White Chocolate & Berries

CHEESECAKE

🍴 MAKES ONE 8 INCH CHEESECAKE

This Baked White Chocolate Cheesecake with Mascarpone and Strawberries might well be my best white chocolate cheesecake to date. Smooth, rich, indulgent, satisfying and quite impressive; if you love white chocolate, this is for you!

It's a simple bake that happily offers you an empty canvas for a topping. For a special occasion, a luxurious vanilla-bean-spiked mascarpone with strawberries seems about right. Ideas race through my head with desserts like this. Mango with slivered pistachios, a salted caramel drizzle, a berry coulis, an espresso ganache. I'm sure you get the drift!

INGREDIENTS

BISCUIT BASE

250 g digestive biscuits
125 g butter, melted, cooled

WHITE CHOCOLATE FILLING

4 eggs
200 g white chocolate, melted
300 g cream cheese, room temperature
400 ml cream
100 g vanilla sugar
2½ tbsp cornflour
½ vanilla bean, scraped

VANILLA MASCARPONE CREAM

150 g mascarpone cheese, chilled
25 g powdered sugar
½ vanilla bean, scraped

METHOD

Place the biscuits in a Ziploc bag and crush.
Stir in the melted butter.
Press into an 8 inch loose-bottomed tin. Place the tin in the freezer.

Preheat the oven to 160°C.
Place all the ingredients for the filling in a bowl of a food processor, and blend on medium speed for a few minutes to mix well. Pour over the crust and bake for an hour.
Cool completely in the oven, then cover and refrigerate overnight.

Place all the ingredients in a large bowl and whisk until just mixed and smooth. Don't over-mix. Spread over the chilled cheesecake and top with the strawberry topping.
Garnish with freshly sliced strawberries and fresh rosemary sprigs.

STRAWBERRY TOPPING

250 g strawberries, chopped
Few sprigs fresh rosemary
100 g sugar
½ vanilla bean, scraped
1 tbsp balsamic vinegar

Place all the ingredients in a non-reactive saucepan. Simmer over low heat until it becomes jam-like and thick. Taste and adjust the sweetness. Discard the rosemary sprig.
Cool completely.

(**Note:** *Can be made a day before.*)

Mini Dark Chocolate

CHEESECAKES

🍴 **MAKES EIGHT 2 INCH CHEESECAKES**

I've had several obsessions over the years, and yet another continues to be creating individual desserts and smaller portions. I really enjoy plating and garnishing them, then serving them up interestingly.

These mini cheesecakes are the first of many individual-portioned desserts, more of which you'll find in the 'Puddings, Trifles & Panna Cotta' section.

Sinful, creamy and simple, this cheesecake is yet another answer to chocolate cravings. If you're looking for a quick bake, perhaps a petite cheesecake, look no further.

INGREDIENTS

BISCUIT BASE

150 g digestive biscuits
30 g cocoa powder
20 g jaggery powder
50 g unsalted butter, chopped, chilled

DARK CHOCOLATE FILLING

3 eggs
200 g dark chocolate, melted
150 g cream cheese, room temperature
150 g mascarpone, room temperature
90 g jaggery powder
30 g cocoa powder
1 tsp vanilla extract

TOPPING

Fresh strawberries
Dark chocolate flakes
Fresh mint, cocoa powder

METHOD

Run the biscuits, cocoa powder and jaggery powder in a blender to fine crumbs.

Alternatively place the biscuits in a Ziploc bag and crush with a rolling pin to make fine crumbs.

Stir in the cocoa powder and jaggery powder, then stir in the melted clarified butter/ghee.

Press into eight individual 2 inch baking rings. Place the rings on a tray and place in the freezer while you get the filling ready.

Preheat the oven to 160°C.

Place all the ingredients for the filling in the bowl of a food processor, and blend well to mix, 1–2 minutes on medium speed.

Ladle the filling into each dessert ring. Bake for approximately 30 minutes, until slightly firm to the touch.

Leave to cool in the oven, then cover with foil and refrigerate overnight.

Gently push out from the ring moulds/baking tin, and plate. Dust with cocoa powder, top with diced strawberries and dark chocolate flakes. Garnish with mint. Serve cold or leave at room temperature for 30 minutes before serving.

*(**Tip:** Use seasonal fruit to top, or whipped cream, salted butter caramel, etc. You can even add a dash of orange liqueur and top with whipped mascarpone!)*

Tiramousse
CHEESECAKE (EGGLESS, NO-BAKE)

♨ MAKES ONE 8 INCH CHEESECAKE

Some desserts show up again and again in my home, and this is one of them. The flavours come together beautifully and the coffee–chocolate pairing really shines. This was my cheesecake twist to the classic Italian tiramisu, a recipe that was made by many when I shared it online. After all, who doesn't love a good tiramisu!

Dessert should be fun to make and fun to serve; and this is a fine example of one!

INGREDIENTS

BISCUIT BASE

125 g digestive biscuits
25 g brown sugar
50 g unsalted butter, melted, cooled

DARK CHOCOLATE MOUSSE LAYER

1 tsp gelatine
25 ml milk, warm
200 ml cream
75 g bittersweet or dark chocolate, chopped fine
30 g brown sugar
25 ml Kahlúa (optional)

COFFEE PANNA COTTA LAYER

1 tsp gelatine
25 ml milk, warm
100 ml cream
50 g brown sugar
10 g instant coffee powder
1 tbsp Kahlúa (optional)
200 g mascarpone

METHOD

Place the biscuits in a Ziploc bag and crush with a rolling pin to make crumbs.
Stir in the sugar and melted butter.
Press into an 8 inch loose-bottomed tin and place in the freezer while you make the filling.

Sprinkle the gelatine over the tepid milk in a small bowl and leave until spongy. Place the bowl in warm water and leave until the gelatine is clear.
Place the cream and sugar in a heavy-bottomed saucepan and whisk well to mix. Simmer over low heat until bubbles begin to appear around the edges, stirring constantly.
Take off heat and stir in the gelatine mix. Add the Kahlúa (if using) and the dark chocolate.
Whisk well to mix, cool for about 30 minutes, then pour over the chilled biscuit crust.

Sprinkle the gelatine over the tepid milk and prepare as above.
Beat the cream, brown sugar, coffee powder and Kahlúa to soft peaks, then gently whisk in the mascarpone until just smooth. Don't overbeat.
Strain in the melted gelatine, and whisk gently to mix.
Pour the filling over the dark chocolate mousse layer and refrigerate overnight to set.

Pipe over with some lightly sweetened mascarpone if desired, and sift over cocoa powder before serving.

Chocolate & Whiskey
CHEESECAKE

🍴 **MAKES ONE 8 INCH CHEESECAKE**

There's no end to the possibilities a basic cheesecake might offer, as well as the infinite flavour pairings. If whiskey is your poison, this cheesecake could fit the bill. The recipe came about for collaboration with a whiskey brand. I love how sometimes a slight twist can elevate a dessert to something more special!

For a non-alcoholic version, you could use a brewed dark coffee in the cheesecake filling, and honey in the ganache. The strawberries can be flavoured with a split vanilla bean.

INGREDIENTS

BISCUIT BASE

150 g digestive biscuits
20 g brown sugar
30 g cocoa powder
75 g unsalted butter, melted, cooled
A pinch of salt

DARK CHOCOLATE WHISKEY FILLING

200 g dark chocolate, chopped fine
150 g cream cheese, room temperature
150 g mascarpone, room temperature
200 ml cream
30 g cocoa powder
3 small eggs
25 ml whiskey
1 tsp vanilla extract
90 g brown sugar

WHISKEY CHOCOLATE GANACHE

100 ml cream
75 g dark chocolate, chopped fine
2 tbsp whiskey
A pinch of salt

WHISKEY-MACERATED STRAWBERRIES

200 g strawberries, quartered
25 g brown sugar
1 tbsp whiskey

METHOD

Run the biscuits, brown sugar and cocoa powder in a blender to fine crumbs. Alternatively, place the biscuits in a Ziploc bag and crush with a rolling pin to make crumbs.
Stir in the sugar and cocoa powder, then stir in the melted clarified butter/ghee.
Press into an 8 inch loose-bottomed tin and place in the freezer while you get the filling ready.

Preheat the oven to 160°C.
Place all the ingredients for the filling in the bowl of a food processor, and blend on medium speed for a few minutes to mix well. Pour over the crust and bake for an hour.
Cool completely in the oven, then refrigerate covered in the fridge, overnight.

Place the chocolate in a glass bowl.
Heat the cream till hot but not boiling and pour over the chocolate.
Allow to stand for 10–15 minutes until the chocolate softens, then stir gently until smooth. Whisk in the whiskey and a pinch of salt.
Cool to a spreadable consistency.
Pour over the cooled cheesecake, then top with whiskey-macerated strawberries, fresh sprigs of thyme, perhaps.

Stir it all together in a glass bowl and allow the flavours to mature for 15–20 minutes.
Strain and top the ganache with the macerated berries.

(**Note:** *The remaining liquid can be added to a chilled beverage, though it's good on its own too!*)

Best Baked Chocolate

CHEESECAKE (EGGLESS)

This was one of the last recipes I baked for this cookbook, one that surprisingly turned out really well for an eggless baked cheesecake. The flavours were deep, each bite smooth and sensuous, and the ganache a welcome addition to the all-round deliciousness.

I baked this in a round 8 inch tin as well as in a heart-shaped mould. Both work well. Feel free to top this with flavours you like. Perhaps salted caramel, coffee or orange zest added to a whipped ganache, or seasonal fruit. As I write, I'm thinking Maltesers and cocoa nibs!

INGREDIENTS

BISCUIT BASE

150 g Marie/Digestive biscuits
75 g clarified butter/ghee, melted, cooled

CHEESECAKE FILLING

100 ml cream
100 g bittersweet chocolate, chopped fine
100 g milk chocolate, chopped fine
1 tbsp instant coffee powder
150 g cream cheese, room temperature
200 g mascarpone, room temperature
50 g thick yogurt, room temperature
15 g cocoa powder
15 g cornstarch
75 g brown sugar
1 tsp vanilla extract
A pinch of salt

METHOD

Preheat the oven to 180°C.
Line the outside of a heart-shaped mould with a double layer of aluminium foil to form a base, and place on a baking tray.
Run the biscuits in a blender to a fine meal or place in a Ziploc bag and crush with a rolling pin to make fine crumbs.
Stir in the melted clarified butter. Press the mix into the mould.
Bake for 12–15 minutes until light golden brown. Cool while you make the filling.
Reduce the oven temperature to 150°C.

Melt the cream with the chocolates over a double boiler (or microwave), and stir until smooth. Stir in the coffee powder.
In the bowl of a stand mixer, add all the other ingredients with the melted chocolate and whisk until smooth. (Alternatively, use a large bowl and an electric hand-mixer.)
Pour the filling into the biscuit shell and smoothen.
Place the tin in the bigger baking tin and fill it up to halfway with warm water.
Bake for an hour, then leave the cheesecake in the oven to cool. Cover and refrigerate overnight.
Top as follows.

CHOCOLATE GANACHE

75 g bittersweet chocolate, chopped fine
150 ml cream

Place the chocolate in a glass bowl.

Heat the cream till hot but not boiling and pour over the chocolate. Allow to stand for 10–15 minutes until the chocolate softens, then stir gently until smooth. Rest at room temperature, whisking on and off, until it is pipeable. Pipe rosettes over the cheesecake.

(*Note: The cheesecake tastes best if allowed to stand at room temperature for 30 minutes before serving. The coffee is optional but it enhances the depth and taste of the chocolate.*)

WHAT IF?

If you want to skip the coffee, you can use grated orange zest for a flavour change.

Puddings, Trifles & Panna Cotta

My personal favourite way to do desserts—fuss-free, make-ahead, infinitely adaptable to individual tastes, and interesting to garnish. The panna cotta and some of the puddings are mostly individual portions and fun to serve in stem glasses. I always make extra portions as there's always someone checking the refrigerator the next day!

Microwave Banana Chocolate
MUG PUDDING FOR TWO (EGGLESS)

MAKES 1 LARGE 450 ML MUG

Another recipe that was born during the lockdown, with my daughter stuck away from home, craving dessert. This one was especially for her since she was fed up of mug cake recipes she found online. It made me discover I could rustle up a quick dessert in the microwave, an option I had never considered!

*Perfect for when you impatiently need a deep dose of chocolatey goodness. Think late nights, friends suddenly showing up, when you just **need** dessert, or cold, wintry nights where pudding is the only warmth you require. For all those times, this is going to hit the spot!*

INGREDIENTS

DRY MIX

45 g wholewheat flour
A pinch of salt
¼ tsp baking soda
30 g walnuts, chopped
40 g dark chocolate chips

WET MIX

85 g bananas or **1** large, ripe banana, mashed
30 g brown sugar
50 g clarified butter/ghee, melted, cooled
25 g thick yogurt
15 g cocoa powder
25 ml milk

TOPPING

Extra walnuts and chocolate chips

METHOD

Whisk together the dry ingredients in a small bowl. Reserve.

In a large glass bowl, whisk together the mashed banana, brown sugar, clarified butter/ghee, yogurt and cocoa powder. Whisk well to mix, then whisk in the milk.

Stir in the reserved dry mix gently. Don't over-mix.

Turn it out into a large microwave-safe mug, top with walnut halves and mini chocolate chips.

Cook on high power for 2½ minutes. Test with a wooden pick. It should come out clean while testing the edge. If not, run it for another 30 seconds.

Stand for 5–10 minutes, then serve immediately.

Serve warm or cold. Tastes nice with a scoop of vanilla ice-cream!

*(**Note:** This is a gooey pudding on the base. If you'd like it a bit firmer, you could cook for 30 seconds more.)*

Hot Chocolate Christmas Cake
PUDDING

🍴 MAKES 6 SERVINGS

The name says it all. Two winter holiday favourites, fruit cake and hot chocolate pudding, met quite happily here, embracing the best of each other. The result was an indulgent pudding with spicy undertones, smothered by a delicately orange-spiked hot chocolate.

It's a recipe that came about while creating content for Cadbury where I had extra hot chocolate on hand after a shoot. If you have leftover fruit cake, this is just what you should do! It makes the holiday season last deliciously longer!

You can also use a 120 g bar of Cadbury Silk, which is what I used originally.

INGREDIENTS

6 large slices of fruit cake

HOT CHOCOLATE CUSTARD

3 tbsp cocoa powder
1 tbsp cornflour
300 ml milk
2 tbsp coconut sugar
Zest of **1** orange
100 g bittersweet chocolate, chopped fine

TOPPING

100 ml cream, chilled, whisked until smooth
Cocoa powder for dusting over
Chocolate shards

METHOD

Mix all the ingredients, except the chocolate, in a heavy-bottomed saucepan, and place over a low flame. Whisk well, stirring constantly. Once it gets to a simmering boil, stir constantly until it becomes creamy and thick. Take off the heat and add the chocolate, stirring until the chocolate has melted.

Divide the crumbled cake between the serving glasses and pour the hot custard over it. Refrigerate for 4 hours, then top with cream. Dust with cocoa powder and garnish with chocolate shards.

(**Note:** *The pudding tastes even better the next day, so it's a great make-ahead option. It keeps well in the fridge for 3–4 days.*)

WHAT IF?

If you don't have fruit cake, you can use any cake, crumbled brownies, pound cake, graham crackers, ladyfingers, etc. Get as creative as you like!

Garam Masala Chocolate
PUDDING (EGGLESS)

MAKES 4–6 SERVINGS

Over time, I have got several requests for a stovetop dessert from readers who don't have ovens. This one was for them, and it quickly became one of the most popular desserts on my blog and on Instagram.

A couple of years ago, I gave the pudding a spicy holiday makeover. Steeped with flavours of garam masala and orange zest, it turned out to be quite special.

INGREDIENTS

375 ml milk
250 ml cream
3 tbsp brown sugar
3 tbsp cocoa powder
2 tbsp cornflour
1 tsp garam masala (page 267)
75 g dark chocolate, chopped
1 tbsp clarified butter/ghee
Zest of **1** orange

METHOD

Put all the ingredients in a heavy-bottomed saucepan. Whisk well to mix until smooth, then simmer over low heat, stirring constantly till the mixture begins to thicken.

Taste and adjust the sweetness if required.

Take off the heat, strain and pour into serving dishes.

Serve immediately or cool, refrigerate for 2–3 hours.

Dust with cocoa powder, and garnish, if desired.

Banana Chocolate

PUDDING (EGGLESS)

🍴 MAKES ONE 8 INCH BAKED PUDDING

This is not a cake, and this is not a pudding; it's a cake pudding. Firm but not set, moist and delicious, this eggless chocolate pudding is an indulgent dessert to serve up. Loaded with the goodness of bananas, wholewheat flour, ghee, chocolate, coconut sugar and walnuts, this is great served hot out of the oven. Interestingly, it tastes nice cold too.

A simple recipe, as always, where a dry mix and wet mix come together to create magic!

INGREDIENTS

DRY MIX

85 g wholewheat flour
35 g cocoa powder
½ tsp baking soda
50 g walnuts, chopped
100 g dark chocolate chips
A pinch of salt

WET MIX

150 g bananas or **2** large, ripe bananas, mashed
65 g coconut sugar
100 g clarified butter/ghee, softened
55 g Greek yogurt
85 g dark chocolate, melted
1 tbsp instant coffee powder
50 ml milk, warm
1 tsp vanilla extract

TOPPING

Extra walnuts and chocolate chips

METHOD

Preheat the oven to 180°C. Lightly grease a round 8 inch baking tin.

Whisk together the dry ingredients in a small bowl. Reserve.

In a large glass bowl, whisk together the bananas, coconut sugar, clarified butter/ghee, Greek yogurt, dark chocolate, coffee powder, milk and vanilla extract until smooth.
Add the reserved dry mix to the wet mix, stirring until just mixed. Don't over-mix.
Transfer the batter to the prepared tin and level out. Top with walnuts and chocolate chips.
Bake for 30 minutes, until a toothpick tester pushed into the edge comes out with a few moist crumbs.
Serve warm or cold.

This pudding tastes really nice with a scoop of vanilla ice-cream!

Spooky Halloween Chocolate
PUDDING

🍴 **MAKES 6 SERVINGS**

Kids love this at Halloween, the chocolate dirt and ghosts bringing Halloween to your dessert table, complete with fondant pumpkins. It's a 'spirited dessert' sans alcohol of another kind for kids! I've made this pudding for years ever since the kids were little. They're grown up now and certainly have no charm for ghosts or Halloween, but I enjoy creating it so much that I make it every year without fail. Boo! The meringue ghosts can be made ahead as they take long to bake at low heat, but you could skip them to keep the dessert egg-free. However, if you are feeling adventurous, you could attempt making aquafaba meringue ghosts.

INGREDIENTS

PUDDING

400 ml milk
200 ml cream
30 g cocoa powder
1 tsp cinnamon powder
35 g quick-cooking oats
150 g dark chocolate, chopped
75 g brown sugar
30 g honey

CHOCOLATE DIRT

120 g packet chocolate Oreo cookies

MERINGUE GHOSTS (MAKES 6-8)

1 egg white
A pinch of cream of tartar
¼ cup icing sugar
A few drops of orange extract
Mini chocolate chips

METHOD

Place all the ingredients in a heavy-bottomed saucepan and simmer over low heat, stirring constantly until the mixture begins to thicken. Once the mixture becomes as thick as custard, take off heat, allow to cool, then puree with an immersion blender or blend in a food processor until smooth.
Pour into serving bowls/glasses.
Cool and then refrigerate for 2–3 hours, or overnight.

Place the cookies in the jar of a blender. Process until you get fine crumbs.
Alternatively, place in a Ziploc bag and crush with a rolling pin.

Preheat the oven to 100°C. Line a cookie tray with parchment paper.
Place the egg white with the cream of tartar in a medium bowl. Beat until the egg white is mousse-like.
Add the sugar, 1 tbsp at a time, and beat on high speed until firm, smooth and glossy. The meringue should hold stiff peaks.
Spoon it into a piping bag fitted with a round nozzle (or cut a ¼ inch bit off to give you a ½ inch hole).
Pipe out little ghosts on to the parchment paper. Place 2 mini chocolate chips for eyes.
Bake for about 1½–2 hours until firm and crisp to the touch.
Leave in the oven to cool completely.
Top the pudding with chocolate dirt, meringue ghosts, fondant pumpkins, etc.

Almond Milk Panna Cotta
FLAN (VEGAN)

MAKES ONE 8 INCH FLAN

Delicious things happen sometimes when you experiment with 'everything but the kitchen sink'! Unfinished portions of almond milk, coconut sugar and dark chocolate led me to make this dessert. I kept it vegan using agar agar, keeping my fingers crossed that it would set. It did, and quite beautifully.

Not your traditional flan, this light dessert is pleasing to the senses, and quite satisfying.

INGREDIENTS

400 ml almond milk
25 g coconut sugar
75 g dark chocolate, chopped
30 g cornflour
30 g cocoa powder
2.5 tsp agar agar

TOPPING

Rose petals, pistachio slivers

METHOD

Whisk all the ingredients together in a heavy-bottomed saucepan. Simmer over low heat until the mixture thickens, whisking constantly. Cool to room temperature, stirring often. Pour into a lightly oiled, silicon mould. Cover with clingwrap and refrigerate to set overnight. Place a plate over the mould and gently but briskly turn over to release.

Garnish with rose petals and pistachio slivers.

WHAT IF?

If you don't have agar agar, you can use an equal amount of gelatine instead.
However, gelatine will not keep the flan vegetarian/vegan.

Silky Chocolate Almond Milk
PUDDING (EGGLESS)

MAKES 4–6 SERVINGS

This pudding brings together silky, smooth chocolate topped with crisp, biscuit-coated chocolate. You can imagine how good the textures and flavours are. Edible spring flowers from the garden prettied them up some more, a perfect example of everything I like about individual portions.

This pudding is a no-brainer—a quick stovetop pudding, vegetarian, with no eggs. Surprisingly enough, it's light like a mousse, yet deeply chocolatey and quite indulgent.

INGREDIENTS

400 ml almond milk
15 g cornflour
25 g cocoa powder
120 g Cadbury Dairy Milk Silk
80 g dark chocolate, chopped
30 g coconut sugar

TOPPING

Chocolate confectionary, sprinkles, nuts, etc.

METHOD

Whisk the first three ingredients well in a heavy-bottomed saucepan. Add both the chocolates and the sugar. Simmer over low heat, whisking constantly, until the chocolate melts and the mixture is thick.

Cool to room temperature, whisking often.

Transfer to serving glasses/bowls and refrigerate to set for 3–4 hours, or overnight.

Top with cookies, chocolate squares, etc.

Smoked Tea & White Chocolate

COCONUT CREAM PANNA COTTA (EGGLESS)

🍴 MAKES 4–6 SERVINGS

Sometimes you need a play of flavours on your palate, and flavours that excite you, that make you want to sink into luxury! This panna cotta hits all those notes. The flavours are deep and extended. First the subtle smokiness of the tea hits the palate, then the sweetness of white chocolate charms you. The coconut undertones are soothing and lilting.

I dreamt of making this dessert one evening after enjoying a cold brew tea created by my dear friend and tea sommelier Anamika Singh. The Pine Wood Smoked Tea is my most loved one from her hand-crafted range of Anandini Himalaya Tea. I am eternally grateful to her for spoiling me with her teas.

INGREDIENTS

2 tsp gelatine
250 ml coconut milk
2 tbsp Anandini Himalaya Pine Wood Smoked Tea
300 ml cream
75 g white chocolate, chopped fine
15 g coconut sugar

METHOD

Steep the coconut milk overnight with the tea leaves in a screwtop bottle, shaking a couple of times. Strain out the steeped coconut milk.
Sprinkle the gelatine over the water in a small bowl and leave until spongy. Place the bowl in warm water and leave until the gelatine is clear.
Place the cream and steeped coconut milk in a heavy-bottomed saucepan.
Add the chocolate and coconut sugar. Simmer over low heat until smooth, 3–5 minutes, stirring constantly.
Take off the heat and stir in the gelatine mix.
Cool to room temperature, then strain and pour into serving moulds. Refrigerate overnight to set.
Loosen the edges with a knife and overturn on to a dessert platter. Alternatively, set in stem glasses.

Chocolate & Whiskey
PANNA COTTA (EGGLESS)

🍴 MAKES 6 SERVINGS

Chocolate is such a good partner to all things fine! Alcohol pairs well with chocolate, and you don't need a lot to create a pleasant dessert. Here, the slight woody, smoky undertones of whiskey blend in quite beautifully with dark chocolate, making my favourite dessert delightfully full-bodied and even more indulgent.

A quenelle of mascarpone to finish it off, a few chocolate flakes, a sprig of mint and frozen blackberries make this a combination worth the indulgence! It's interesting to see the subtle notes come together so elegantly.

INGREDIENTS

2½ tsp gelatine
120 ml milk, warm
500 ml cream
150 g dark chocolate, chopped
120 g brown sugar
2 tbsp whiskey

METHOD

Sprinkle the gelatine over the milk in a small bowl and leave until spongy. Place the bowl in warm water and leave until the gelatine is clear.

Meanwhile, place the chocolate, cream and brown sugar into a heavy-bottomed saucepan and simmer over gentle heat, stirring constantly. Take off the heat when small bubbles begin to appear around the edges at the bottom. Stir in the gelatine mix and whiskey. Taste and adjust the sugar if desired.

Cool to room temperature, then strain and pour into serving glasses/bowls/moulds. Refrigerate overnight to set.

Gently dip the bottom in warm water, loosen the edges with a knife and overturn on to a small serving plate. Alternatively, set in stem glasses.

You could pour unsweetened single cream on top for a colour variation and add berries if you like. Finish with a dusting of chocolate shavings.

Chocolate Brownie Coffee
KAHLÚA TRIFLE (EGGLESS)

MAKES ONE 4 INCH TRIFLE

I have a confession to make. I sometimes make wholegrain brownies just so I can make a trifle. Brownies get over really fast at home, so I sneak some away before they become history.

Brownies soaked in a coffee Kahlúa syrup, layered and topped with a barely sweetened coffee whipped cream, is everything you might ask for in a trifle if you love coffee! Use either the eggless brownies or the dark chocolate ones in the traybake section. Also, if coffee is not your thing, think vanilla bean Chantilly, an orange-flavoured cream, maybe peppermint for the holidays; make the trifle your own!

INGREDIENTS

100 ml cream, chilled
100 g mascarpone, chilled
30 g icing sugar (to taste)
1 tbsp instant coffee powder
2–3 tbsp Kahlúa
4–6 dark chocolate brownies, broken or diced (page 87)

METHOD

With an electric hand-beater, whip both the creams with the coffee powder and icing sugar until just smooth. Don't over-beat.

Taste and adjust the sweetness. You'll need it mildly sweet because the brownies are sweet too.

Begin layering with 2–3 brownies, as per dish size. You can do individual portions or one large trifle.

Place ⅓ of the brownies in a serving dish.

Drizzle over with some Kahlúa, then add a layer of mascarpone coffee cream. Repeat.

Refrigerate for at least an hour for the flavours to mature.

TOPPING

Chocolate flakes, cocoa powder or cocoa nibs.

Top with chocolate flakes, cocoa powder or cocoa nibs.

WHAT IF?

If you don't have Kahlúa, you can use a sweetened brewed coffee instead.

Dark Chocolate & Cherry
CHIA SEED PUDDING (EGGLESS)

MAKES 4 SERVINGS

Do you sometimes wish you could make a season last forever? That's just how I feel about summer, when stone fruits like cherries, peaches and apricots are in plenty. This dessert reminds me of the goodness of summer, and how so little can make you feel so happy. You'll find several references to cherries with chocolate across the book. Cherries are one of my favourite stone fruits, and I absolutely love how beautifully they pair with chocolate.

INGREDIENTS

250 ml coconut milk
3 tbsp cocoa powder
3 tbsp coconut sugar
2 tbsp chia seeds

METHOD

Place the ingredients in a glass bowl and whisk well to mix.
Stand for 15 minutes for the seeds to swell up, then whisk again.
Ladle into serving glasses/bowls and refrigerate for a couple of hours.
Top with balsamic cherries, fresh cherries and mint.

TOPPING

200 g balsamic cherries
(page 259)
Fresh cherries
Sprigs of mint

WHAT IF?

If you don't have cherries, you can use strawberries or blueberries instead.

Dark Chocolate & Coffee Cream
SET PUDDING (EGGLESS)

♨ MAKES 4–6 SERVINGS

Agar agar was something new to me, an ingredient discovered at the same time I began eggless baking. I was quite happy using gelatine but as the chant for plant-based jelly recipes grew, I began pushing my boundaries.

It's amazing how much you learn when you interact with community, how many more chocolate desserts see the light of day.

INGREDIENTS

550 ml milk
100 ml cream
2 tbsp cocoa powder
75 g brown sugar
100 g dark chocolate, chopped
1 tsp agar agar

METHOD

Place the milk, cream, cocoa powder, sugar and agar agar in a heavy-bottomed saucepan and whisk until smooth.
Place over low heat and bring to a simmering boil for about 5 minutes. Stir constantly.
Pour this mixture into dessert jars, bowls, glasses, etc.
Cool to room temperature, then strain and pour into serving moulds. Refrigerate for 2–3 hours until to set.

WHIPPED KAHLÚA COFFEE-CREAM

100 ml cream, chilled
100 g cream cheese, room temperature
1 tbsp instant coffee powder
1 tbsp powdered sugar
1 tbsp Kahlúa (optional)

With an electric beater, beat all the ingredients for the whipped cream together until just smooth.
Pipe over the set pudding. Refrigerate until ready to serve.

Dark Chocolate

PANNA COTTA (EGGLESS)

MAKES 6–8 SERVINGS

We never tire of panna cotta at home. It is one of my most requested desserts made on repeat. Luxurious, soul-satisfying, pretty to serve and ever so simple to make. If you are looking for a make-ahead dessert which is a crowd-pleaser, try this. The recipe is easily doubled and is absolutely wonderful served in chai glasses or cognac glasses, both lending their own charm to this sweetened cream-base dessert.

INGREDIENTS

2½ tsp gelatine
125 ml whole milk, warm
500 ml cream
150 g dark chocolate, chopped
120 g brown sugar

TOPPING

Seasonal berries

METHOD

Sprinkle the gelatine over the water in a small bowl and leave until spongy. Place the bowl in warm water and leave until the gelatine is clear.

Meanwhile, put the chocolate, cream and brown sugar in a heavy-bottomed saucepan and simmer over gentle heat. Stir the cream mixture and take off the heat when small bubbles begin to appear around the edges at the bottom. Stir in the gelatine mix. Taste and adjust the sugar if desired.

Cool to room temperature, then strain and pour into serving moulds. Refrigerate overnight to set.

Loosen the edges with a knife and overturn on to a dessert platter. Alternatively, set in stem glasses.

You could pour unsweetened cream on top for a colour variation, and add berries if you like.

Chocolate & Salted Caramel
MOUSSE-A-COTTA (EGGLESS)

MAKES 4–6 SERVINGS

Unfamiliar as the name might sound, this dessert was born out of a previously failed chocolate panna cotta recipe. That Cocoa Mousse-a-Cotta turned out to be one of my most popular recipes and images, especially on Instagram. Turned out the panna cotta didn't set well at all, yet it tasted absolutely delicious. Here, a silky, dark chocolate mousse meets the panna cotta, resulting in a sublime, deep, chocolatey treat. A topping of salted caramel sauce is just the right thing for it.

If you want to skip the salted caramel sauce, you can always add a spoon or two of Kahlúa or Baileys to the mousse. Alternatively, a topping of cream, sweetened or otherwise, whipped or not, never hurts.

INGREDIENTS

1 tsp gelatine
50 ml milk, warm
500 ml cream
25 g cocoa powder
50 g brown sugar
100 g dark chocolate, chopped

METHOD

Sprinkle the gelatine over the milk in a small bowl and leave until spongy. Place the bowl in warm water and leave until the gelatine is clear.

Place cream, sugar and cocoa powder in a heavy-bottomed saucepan and whisk well to mix.

Simmer over low heat until bubbles begin to appear around the edges, stirring constantly, else the cocoa will get lumpy.

Take off the heat and stir in the gelatine mix and dark chocolate. Whisk well to mix. Cool to room temperature, then strain and pour into serving jars. Refrigerate overnight to set.

TOPPING

Salted caramel sauce
(page 255)
Chocolate shards (page 129)

Top with salted caramel sauce and chocolate shards before serving.

Dark Chocolate & Coffee
PANNA COTTA (EGGLESS)

¶¶ MAKES 6 SERVINGS

Another 'dessert in a glass', yet another panna cotta, chocolate with coffee again! The coffee–chocolate pairing really rules my world, makes me happy, and is super indulgent too.

INGREDIENTS

DARK CHOCOLATE CREAM

300 ml cream
125 g bittersweet chocolate, chopped
25 g cocoa powder
25 g honey
10 ml Kahlúa (optional)

COFFEE PANNA COTTA

2 tsp gelatine
125 ml milk, warm
300 ml cream
1½ tbsp instant coffee powder
100 g brown sugar

TOPPING

Chocolate curls/shards

METHOD

Place the cream, cocoa powder, chocolate and honey in a heavy-bottomed saucepan. Whisk well, then simmer until smooth and the chocolate has melted.
Whisk in the Kahlúa, if using.
Place 6 wine glasses at a slant in a loaf tin and pour the chocolate mixture into them. Leave these to set in the fridge for 2–3 hours till they hold shape.

Sprinkle the gelatine over the 2 tbsp of milk in a small bowl and leave until spongy. Place the bowl in warm water and leave until the gelatine is clear.
Meanwhile, put the cream, remaining milk, sugar and coffee powder in a saucepan and bring to a simmering boil over low heat. Simmer for 5 minutes.
Take the cream mixture off heat, whisk in the gelatine until mixed uniformly. Adjust the sweetness, if required.
Strain and cool to room temperature and then pour over the set dark chocolate mousse.
Refrigerate overnight until set.

Top with dark chocolate curls, dusted with cocoa powder.

White Chocolate & Coffee
PANNA COTTA (EGGLESS)

🍴 MAKES 6 SERVINGS

Indulgent, indulgent, indulgent! If coffee pairs well with dark chocolate, it works equally well with white chocolate. If you are a coffee lover like me, you'll probably love all the different ways you can pair these two ingredients. The addition of a good-quality white chocolate adds depth and body to the panna cotta, a different sweetness too. This is one you are going to love!

INGREDIENTS

2 tsp gelatine
100 ml milk, warm
100 g white chocolate, chopped
400 ml cream
25 g brown sugar
2 tbsp instant coffee powder

METHOD

Sprinkle the gelatine over the 2 tbsp of water in a small bowl and leave until spongy. Place the bowl in warm water and leave until the gelatine is clear.

Meanwhile, put the white chocolate, milk, cream, brown sugar and coffee powder into a heavy-bottomed saucepan, and simmer over gentle heat.

Stir constantly for 5 minutes, then take off the heat when small bubbles begin to appear around the edges at the bottom. Stir in the gelatine mix. Strain and taste and adjust the sugar if desired.

Cool to room temperature, then strain and pour into serving glasses. Refrigerate overnight to set.

Brownie Fudge
PUDDING CAKE

MAKES ONE 8 INCH PUDDING CAKE

This fudgy chocolate pudding cake comes together as easily as can be. It is quite the most comforting thing ever; a dessert served warm with vanilla ice-cream, or by itself too. It's inspired by a pudding cake my amazing friend Ruchira baked for us when we dropped by unannounced one day. She eyeballed ingredients, randomly throwing them into a large bowl while talking to us, hand-mixing away busily with one whisk of a hand-beater. Then a short while later, just like that, we were served dessert!

INGREDIENTS

DRY MIX

130 g wholewheat flour
50 g cocoa powder
½ tsp baking soda
A pinch of salt
50 g walnuts, chopped
100 g dark chocolate chips

WET MIX

100 g unsalted butter, melted, cooled
1 egg
50 g Greek yogurt
100 g brown sugar
120 ml milk
60 ml cream

METHOD

Preheat the oven to 180°C.

Whisk together the dry ingredients in a small bowl. Reserve.

In a large bowl, whisk all the ingredients well.
Fold the reserved dry mix into the wet mix.
Transfer to a round 8 inch baking tin.
Bake for 25–30 minutes. It'll still be slightly jiggly in the centre, don't overbake it.
Allow to sit for about 15–20 minutes.
Serve warm with ice-cream, perhaps a drizzle of caramel syrup and toasted walnut halves.

WHAT IF?

If you don't have Greek yogurt, you can use thick/hung yogurt instead.

Dark Chocolate & Pumpkin
WALNUT OAT PUDDING
(EGGLESS, GLUTEN-FREE)

MAKES 6 GLASSES

This pudding has everything and more in it, yet is eggless and gluten-free. It's also loaded with the goodness of walnuts, an ingredient I love to use while baking. I was fortunate to have experienced the walnut harvest tour in Lodi, California, with California Walnuts India, the first time I ever saw walnuts growing on trees! This was one of the recipes that came about while working with them.

This is a really quick pudding, soft set yet set enough to carry walnuts and seasonal fruit on top! I find the gentle goodness of home-made pumpkin puree paired with cinnamon and chocolate quite appealing. The great thing is that you can sneak the vegetable into your kids' desserts and they'll never guess!

INGREDIENTS

PUDDING

250 ml cream
75 g pumpkin puree
(page 264)
1 tsp cinnamon powder
30 g cocoa powder
40 g quick-cooking oats
150 g dark chocolate, chopped
fine
75 g brown sugar
50 g honey
75 g toasted walnuts, chopped

TOPPING

Toasted walnut halves,
persimmon slices,
organic rose petals, etc.

METHOD

Place all the ingredients, except the walnuts, in a heavy-bottomed saucepan, whisk well and simmer over low heat, stirring constantly until it begins to thicken. Once it becomes as thick as a custard, take the pan off the heat and cool to room temperature.
Stir in the chopped walnuts and then ladle into serving glasses/bowls. Refrigerate for 2–3 hours, or overnight.

Top with toasted walnut halves, fresh seasonal fruit like figs, persimmons and candied pumpkin. Sprinkle over a few organic rose petals or pomegranate pearls for a pop of colour.

Self-Saucing Chocolate & Walnut
PUDDING (EGGLESS)

I have the most fun when I plan make-ahead desserts. The first bit of this dessert sits in the fridge overnight to rest. About an hour before time to serve, it needs a dose of brown sugar and cocoa powder scattered over the top, some boiling water, and into the oven it goes. Then almost effortlessly, pudding's ready as dinner's done! It's best served warm out of the oven to enjoy the sauce at the bottom. As it sits, it gently absorbs the sauce but is still good, moist and comforting when reheated.

INGREDIENTS

PUDDING

DRY MIX

100 g all-purpose flour
25 g wholewheat flour
75 g coconut sugar
2 tsp baking powder
2 tbsp cocoa powder
100 g walnuts, chopped
A pinch of salt

WET MIX

125 ml milk
50 g clarified butter/ghee
75 g condensed milk

TOPPING

75 g brown sugar
75 g coconut sugar
2 tbsp cocoa powder
250 ml boiling water

METHOD

Grease a 1 litre baking dish with melted clarified butter/ghee.

Whisk together the dry ingredients in a small bowl. Reserve.

Put the milk and condensed milk in a large bowl. Heat the clarified butter/ghee and add to the bowl. Whisk well to mix.

Add the reserved dry mix to the wet mix, stirring just well enough to blend.

Pour into the prepared baking dish.

Cover the dish with clingwrap and refrigerate overnight.

About an hour before serving time, preheat the oven to 180°C.

Stir together the ingredients for the topping in a bowl.

Take off the clingwrap and sprinkle the topping mix over the cold unbaked pudding.

Pour the boiling water over the topping mix and bake for 30–35 minutes until crusty, puffy and firm in the centre.

Serve with unsweetened cream or vanilla/cinnamon ice-cream.

*(**Note:** You can make it in a loaf tin, if you have nothing else. A Borosil bake-and-serve works really well here too.)*

Dark Chocolate & Strawberries
SET PUDDING (EGGLESS)

⛶ MAKES 4 SERVINGS

In north India, we are blessed with fresh strawberries through winter, then through early summer again. Each time strawberry season arrives, like a child, I'm over the moon. I love creating desserts around strawberries, and happily, they pair really well with chocolate. This pudding is interesting, with deep underlying notes of macerated strawberries with thyme. It's like a strawberry version of the black forest cake without the cake! The dash of Cointreau added to this dessert is quite optional yet most delightful.

INGREDIENTS

PUDDING

300 ml cream
125 g bittersweet chocolate, chopped
1 tbsp Cointreau (optional)
1 tbsp clarified butter/ghee
1 tbsp honey

STRAWBERRY TOPPING

200 g strawberries, diced
2 tbsp light brown sugar
Dash of lime juice
1 tbsp Cointreau (optional)
A few sprigs of fresh thyme

METHOD

Place the chocolate in a glass bowl. Heat the cream till hot but not boiling and pour over the chocolate. Allow to stand for 10–15 minutes until the chocolate softens.

Add the clarified butter/ghee, honey and Cointreau and stir until smooth.

Allow to cool. Once it is firm, whip with an electric hand-beater until light and moussey.

Stir all the strawberries, sugar and lime juice and leave to stand for about 30 minutes to macerate. Strain the liquid out and heat the strained liquid over low heat to reduce, then cool.

Divide the macerated strawberries into two halves. Pour the syrup over one half with the Cointreau. Leave the other half as is.

ASSEMBLE

Divide the half with the reduced syrup between 4 serving glasses/bowls and top with the mousse.

Refrigerate for about an hour. Top with the remaining strawberry topping and garnish with thyme.

Black Forest Crumble
TRIFLE (EGGLESS)

MAKES 4–6 SERVINGS

I'm happiest pottering around the kitchen playing with recipes I've created in the past. As I contemplated baking the Two-Minute Wholegrain Microwave Cookies (page 114) into a biscuit base for a pudding, an idea formed in my head. One thing led to another, and this black forest cherry trifle happened. The trifle has several layers and might look like a tedious recipe on first glance. Break it up and you'll find it quite simple. Cookie crumble, cherry pie filling, almond cream and a chocolate layer, each take 5 minutes if you have mise en place. I was pleasantly surprised when I shared this recipe on Instagram and so many people were inspired to make it.

You could always do a simple layered store-bought cookie crumb and cherry trifle if you're short on time, but this dessert from scratch is well worth the extra two-minute microwave cookie crumble!

INGREDIENTS

WHOLEWHEAT COOKIE CRUMBLE

DRY MIX

75 g wholewheat flour
75 g quick-cooking oats
45 g brown sugar
45 g vanilla sugar (or plain sugar)
1 tsp baking powder
½ tsp baking soda
A pinch of salt
50 g dark chocolate chips
50 g walnuts, chopped

WET MIX

50 g clarified butter/ghee, room temperature
50 g yogurt

METHOD

Whisk together the dry ingredients in a large bowl. Reserve.

Whisk the clarified butter/ghee with the yogurt.
Add the wet mix to the dry mix. Gently combine the two to get a crumbly texture.
Loosely scatter into a microwave-safe flat dish and cook on full power for 3 minutes to make the crumble. Gently loosen into crumbs with a fork.
Repeat for 30 seconds at a time if required. Cool completely.

CHERRY PIE FILLING

400 g cherries, pitted
75 g brown sugar
50 ml water
Juice of **1** lime
½ vanilla bean shell (optional)
1 tbsp corn flour dissolved
in 1 tbsp water
1 tbsp Kirsch (optional)

Simmer the cherries, sugar, water and vanilla bean for 5–7 minutes until the cherries are soft.
Stir in the cornflour mix and cook until thick, stirring constantly.
Take off heat and stir in Kirsch. Cool completely, then refrigerate. Discard the vanilla bean before layering.

WHIPPED ALMOND CREAM

200 ml cream, chilled
30 g icing sugar
A few drops almond extract

Beat the ingredients for the almond cream together on high speed to medium soft peaks.

CHOCOLATE LAYER

200 ml cream
90 g dark chocolate, chopped fine
1 tbsp Kirsch (optional)

Place the chocolate in a glass bowl. Heat the cream till hot but not boiling and pour over the chocolate. Allow to stand for 10–15 minutes until the chocolate softens, then stir gently until smooth. Stir in the Kirsch and allow to cool.

ASSEMBLE (IN A LARGE TRIFLE BOWL)

Put half the cookie crumble at the base of the trifle bowl.
Top with three quarters of the chilled cherry pie filling.
Top with the chocolate layer, then the remaining crumble, followed by the whipped cream, and finally the remaining cherry pie filling.

Truffles, Fudge & Bark

Nothing screams holiday season more than truffles and fudge. Nothing makes for better gifts too. Upcycle jars and pretty tins, add a touch of burlap, maybe a ribbon or a lace trim, to box these edible gifts. I have to ensure I make double batches; one set for home and another to box up. They're also great for a quick, portion-control, guilt-free indulgence when the sweet tooth craves chocolate.

All the recipes under this section are eggless.

Dark Chocolate & Pumpkin
WALNUT TRUFFLES

MAKES 16 (APPROX.)

It was around Halloween in 2018 that we landed in San Francisco with California Walnuts India for the walnut harvest festival. Pumpkin fields, pumpkin décor and pumpkin on the menu reignited my love for this versatile, humble squash. Back from that trip, I created several walnut- and pumpkin-based desserts as part of the association. These truffles were one of them.

This is another way to use walnuts, fresh pumpkin puree and dark chocolate during the festive season. The truffles turned out surprisingly delicious. No added sugar, gluten-free, festive and indulgent, and yes, simple as can be!

INGREDIENTS

150 g bittersweet chocolate, chopped fine
75 g fresh, warm pumpkin puree (page 264)
60 ml cream
1 tbsp cocoa powder
1 tsp pumpkin pie spice
75 g walnuts, chopped

TOPPING

125 g dark chocolate, melted

METHOD

Place the chocolate in a large bowl with the fresh, warm pumpkin puree, cocoa powder and pie spice.
Warm the cream to tepid and pour over the chocolate.
Whisk with a spatula or balloon whisk continuously until the chocolate melts and is smooth. Stir in the walnuts.
Cover the bowl with clingwrap, and refrigerate for 2–3 hours or until firm to the touch.
Using a cookie scoop or round measuring spoon, portion out approximately 16 bits. With very clean hands, roll into balls.

Gently toss into the melted chocolate with a fork to coat. Place on a parchment paper lined sheet and refrigerate until set.
You could toss in a few chocolate non-pareils, shredded coconut, cocoa powder, etc., as well, pressing gently.

WHAT IF?

If you don't have pumpkin pie spice, you can add cinnamon powder or garam masala instead.

Dark Chocolate Garam Masala
FRUIT MINCE TRUFFLES

🍴 MAKES 14–16

A touch of spice can elevate the simplest of recipes to something special. The Indian garam masala adds a unique twist to desserts, the quintessential spice mix finding new use in my kitchen. It might seem an odd addition, somewhat misplaced, as it's a curry or stir-fry ingredient, but bear with me. Garam masala works beautifully in desserts. The spices and sweet ingredients create a fine balance, in many ways bringing out the best in each other, so do give it a shot.

These truffles are vegetarian, eggless, with no added sugar, gluten-free, healthy and make-ahead too. The recipe seems to tick all the boxes for spirited dessert bites. You can always use orange juice to make it sans alcohol. See? Another box ticked off!

If you have extra fruit mince over the holidays, this is an easy and delicious way to use it.

INGREDIENTS

280 g dark chocolate, chopped fine
180 ml cream
¾ cup of leftover garam masala fruit mince (quick recipe below)

GARAM MASALA FRUIT MINCE

150 g dried fruit (mix of fruit like currants, raisins, candied ginger, candied orange peel, dried cranberries, dried blueberries)
1 tsp garam masala (page 267)
15 ml brandy, whiskey, rum (or orange juice)
Zest of ½ an orange

TOPPING

2 tbsp cocoa powder

METHOD

Chop candied ginger and orange peel in a food processor. Place in a large bowl and stir in the remaining ingredients for the fruit mince. Mix to coat well. Clingwrap tightly and leave overnight. Alternatively, microwave for 1 minute, then cover and leave for an hour.

Place the chocolate in a glass bowl. Heat the cream till hot but not boiling and pour over the chocolate. Allow to stand for 10–15 minutes until the chocolate softens, then stir gently until smooth. Whisk in the fruit mince.
Cover the bowl with clingwrap and refrigerate for 2–3 hours or until firm to the touch.
Using a cookie scoop or round measuring spoon, portion out approximately 16 bits.
With very clean hands, roll into balls, then toss in the cocoa powder, rolling gently to smoothen.
Refrigerate until cold.

WHAT IF?

If you want to make these vegan, you can use vegan chocolate, almond milk or coconut cream/milk.

Chocolate Rose & Pistachio

BONBONS

MAKES 15

The charm of rose and pistachio is woven into our beautiful culture, and anything with these two ingredients makes things festive. Once again, I love it when something so simple looks so pretty and tastes good too. These keep well in a cool place (or in an airtight box in the fridge in summer). They are another great gifting option too. After all, who doesn't love chocolate!

INGREDIENTS

150 g dark chocolate, chopped fine
1 tbsp pure maple syrup/honey
1 tsp extra virgin olive oil
50 g pistachios roasted, chopped

TOPPING

Pistachio slivers
Rose petals

METHOD

Place the chocolate in a large, dry glass bowl and melt using the double-boiler method.

Alternatively, melt it in the microwave at 30-second intervals. Stir until smooth.

Stir in the remaining ingredients.

Put a few pistachio slivers and rose petals into each cavity of a 15-hole silicon mould and divide the mix between the cavities.

Refrigerate for a couple of hours until set. Demould and store in a cool place.

Earthy Date & Nuts
ENERGY BALLS

🍴 MAKES 10-12

The sweetness of dates pairs really well with cocoa powder. Call these energy balls, protein bites or bliss balls, these no-sugar, nutrient-dense snack or dessert bites pack quite a punch. I absolutely loved how these turned out. Smooth, earthy, flavourful and guilt-free. Use coconut oil or any oil of your choice to make these vegan. They are naturally sweetened. You could always dip them into melted chocolate for more indulgence.

INGREDIENTS

130 g whole almonds
175 g pitted dates
1 tbsp chia seeds
1 tbsp clarified butter/ghee
2 tbsp cocoa powder

METHOD

Deseed and soak the dates in warm water for about 15 minutes. Then strain and discard the water. If using Mejdool dates, you can skip this step.

Run the almonds in the processor/dry grinder briefly to get a rough breadcrumb-like mix. I keep my almonds frozen for this. Don't over process or the almonds will leave oil.

Add the softened dates, chia seeds, ghee and cocoa powder to the processor, and process until the mixture comes together in a sticky lot. Divide into 10–12 portions and roll into balls.

Store in a cool place for a few days, or in an airtight container in the fridge.

Dark Chocolate & Granola
HOLIDAY BARK

MAKES 12-15

If you like to make quick home-made edible gifts for festivals or over the holidays, then this might be a great option. A handful of ingredients, no particular expertise required, yet so much prettiness and great taste on the other side.

INGREDIENTS

200 g dark chocolate, chopped fine
75 g toasted oats granola
50 g pistachios, chopped

TOPPING

Pistachio slivers
Dried rose petals

METHOD

Line a baking tray with parchment paper.
Place the chocolate in a large, dry glass bowl and melt using the double-boiler method.
Alternatively, melt it in the microwave at 30-second intervals. Stir until smooth.
Stir the granola and chopped pistachios into the melted chocolate.
Pour over the parchment paper and spread into a rectangle using an offset spatula.
Sprinkle the top with organic rose petals and pistachio slivers.
Place in the refrigerator to set completely for about 15 minutes, then break into pieces.
Store in a cool place in winter, or in the fridge in an airtight box in summer.

WHAT IF?

If you don't have granola, you can make these with chopped, salted pistachios and a sprinkling of rose petals.

Dark Chocolate & Cranberry
WALNUT FUDGE

MAKES 64

Come, let's make the easiest fudge ever! It's a two-ingredient recipe, four if you like to add nuts and dried berries like I do. It's one I make every winter, so simple that I almost didn't share it! It might be pertinent here to share the experience of a follower on Instagram who made this recipe using compound chocolate and the fudge didn't set. At the risk of repeating myself, do make sure you use couverture chocolate. I use a 72% chocolate that I think works best, though you can use a 54% chocolate as well. Anything less might make it a little too sweet! Also, topping options are the most fun here: mini marshmallows, salted peanuts, pistachios, hazelnuts, mini pretzels, freeze-dried berries, mini chocolate chips.

*(**Note:** Best kept in the fridge in an airtight box in summer, though I think it's better suited to winter.)*

INGREDIENTS

1 tin (400 g) sweetened condensed milk
400 g bittersweet chocolate, chopped fine
50 g toasted walnuts, chopped
35 g dried cranberries, chopped

METHOD

Line an 8 x 8 inch loose-bottomed tin with parchment paper.
Place the chocolate in a large, dry glass bowl and melt using the double-boiler method.
Alternatively, melt it in the microwave at 30-second intervals. Stir until smooth.
Pour the condensed milk over it.
Whisk gently but swiftly to mix. Once smooth, immediately pour into the prepared tin.
Top with toasted walnuts and cranberries, gently pressing into place.
Refrigerate for 2–3 hours until set.
Cut into squares using a sharp, heavy knife.
Store in a cool place or in the fridge if the weather is warm.

Dark Chocolate Prune & Orange
TRUFFLES

🍴 MAKES 12-15

I often get requests for recipes that use natural sweeteners but specifically 'not dates'. This is for those of you who either don't like dates or are looking for an alternative. Skip the liqueur and make them for kids. Prunes are a powerhouse of nutrition, so see these go down like magic. Dried prunes soaked in fresh orange juice with a dash of zest, toasted walnuts, crystallized ginger powder, maybe some orange liqueur like Cointreau, bring these together quite nicely. Perfect for the dessert platter, for gifting too, like most truffles these are vegetarian and gluten-free, super easy to make.

INGREDIENTS

125 g pitted dried prunes
1 tbsp Grand Marnier
A few drops of orange extract
100 g dark chocolate, chopped fine
125 ml cream
1 tbsp crystallized ginger powder, optional

METHOD

Microwave the prunes with the Grand Marnier and orange extract for 30 seconds or warm the liqueur slightly and add to the prunes. Cover with foil and leave to stand overnight

Place the chocolate in a glass bowl. Heat the cream till hot but not boiling and pour over the chocolate. Allow to stand for 10–15 minutes until the chocolate softens, then stir gently until smooth. Repeat twice after every 20 minutes.

Place the soaked prunes with any liquid in a manual smart chopper/blender with 2–3 tbsp of the chocolate mix. Process until smooth. Add this back to the remaining chocolate in the bowl with the crystallized ginger powder, if using. Stir well with a spatula to mix. Refrigerate for an hour or so until it's firm enough to roll into balls.

Drop teaspoonfuls, one at a time into cocoa powder (or sprinkles, etc.), shake to coat and roll into balls.

Refrigerate until firm, then toss in the cocoa powder once again.

WHAT IF?

If you don't have Grand Marnier or any orange liqueur, you can use an equal amount of orange juice instead.

Chocolate & Blueberry
GREEK YOGURT TRUFFLES

🍴 MAKES 12

These were inspired by ingredients on hand and the need for dessert. They turned out rather nice and quite guilt-free. Berries and chocolate are always good together!

INGREDIENTS

175 g dark chocolate, chopped fine
1 tbsp clarified butter/ghee, melted, cooled
90 g blueberry Greek yogurt
25 g dried blueberries
25 g cocoa powder

METHOD

Place the chocolate in a large, dry glass bowl and melt using the double-boiler method.

Alternatively, melt it in the microwave at 30-second intervals. Stir until smooth.

Allow the chocolate to cool a little, then whisk in the Greek yogurt and clarified butter/ghee.

Refrigerate for about 30 minutes or until firm enough to scoop into balls.

Divide into walnut-sized portions using a cookie scoop or tbsp measure, put a few dried blueberries in the centre of each truffle, roll into balls, then gently toss in the cocoa powder.

Granolas & Parfaits

There was a time when healthy and delicious were considered mutually exclusive concepts. Not any more! Chocolate is healthy, chocolate is delicious, and if the two can come together, nothing like it. Whether it is dessert for breakfast, or breakfast for dessert, here's more chocolate to fuel your day!

All the recipes under this section are eggless.

Nutty Dark Chocolate

GRANOLA

MAKES 800 GRAMS

Granola and toasted cereal are ideal to have on hand for a quick snack, to top yogurt and fruit with, to make granola bars, or even to make a layered fruit parfait. The 1960s saw the 'hippie' movement and a revival of natural, healthy foods in everyday diet, and a shunning of processed and sugary foods. I had forgotten how easy granola, the 'hippie' food of the '60s, was to make at home. Once I started, it firmly became part of my weekend baking routine. I felt like a mad scientist tossing different ingredients into a large bowl, then baking the batch, creating my own mixes. This dark chocolate version was one such result.

Full of fibre, crisp, sweet, buttery too, homemade granola always pleases! You can always substitute the ghee for butter, or maybe a nut butter, honey with maple syrup, play around with different grains, nuts and seeds, or stir in some spice. Go ahead, make it into the granola you love!

INGREDIENTS

DRY MIX

350 g whole rolled oats
125 g walnuts, chopped
25 g cocoa nibs
20 g chia seeds
40 g coconut sugar
½ tsp sea salt

WET MIX

100 g honey
50 g clarified butter/ghee
35 g cocoa powder
½ vanilla bean, scraped

ADD INS (OPTIONAL)
Chocolate chips, dried berries

METHOD

Preheat oven to 180°C. Line a baking tray with parchment paper.

Place all the dry ingredients in a large bowl and stir well.

Whisk together the clarified butter/ghee, honey, cocoa powder and scraped vanilla bean.
Pour the wet mix over the dry mix and stir well, making sure all the ingredients are well-coated with the wet mix.
Turn on to the baking sheet and spread out evenly.
Bake for approximately 25–30 minutes, stirring with a wooden spoon a few times to make sure that the granola cooks evenly. If you like a few clumps, then press it down gently half way through baking.
Once the granola is light golden and fragrant, allow to cool completely on the cooling rack, then break into clumps.
Add the dried berries and chocolate chips, then transfer to an airtight container.
Store in a cool place.

Stovetop Chocolate
TOASTED GRANOLA

MAKES 500 GRAMS

This is generally the batch I make in a hurry when I see that someone's visited the granola jar and it's empty! When you are short on time, maybe don't have an oven, this stovetop small-batch version is a good option. Also, use a nice heavy-bottomed pan or a cast iron skillet to slowly roast the dry ingredients. Show them a little love and they'll reward you beautifully! I often serve this as a granola bowl with a non dairy coconut yogurt, sometimes as a layered parfait with seasonal berries or with bananas and dried cranberries.

INGREDIENTS

DRY MIX

180 g whole rolled oats
70 g mixed seeds
70 g walnuts, chopped
3 tbsp chia seeds
25g clarified butter/ghee
30 g brown sugar
1 tbsp honey
1 tsp cinnamon powder

ADD INS

50 g dried berries or raisins
50 g chocolate chips

METHOD

In a large bowl, stir together the oats, mixed seeds, nuts, chia seeds and cinnamon powder.

Dry roast the above in a heavy-bottomed frying pan or cast-iron skillet over very low heat till the oats appear toasted and light golden. Stir often.

Add the clarified butter/ghee and dry roast for 2–3 minutes, stirring constantly.

Add in the brown sugar and give it a good stir, then drizzle in the honey, mixing well to coat. Roast, stirring often, for another 2–3 minutes, and take off the heat and cool completely on a flat tray.

Stir in the dried berries and chocolate chips and transfer to an airtight container.

WHAT IF?

If you want a vegan option, you can use olive oil, maple syrup and vegan chocolate chips instead.

No-Bake Chocolate Granola
DOUGHNUTS

MAKES 12 MINI DOUGHNUTS

Who doesn't like a cheat doughnut? Not fried, not even baked, yet covered in chocolate, it's a granola doughnut. All you need is a simple silicon doughnut mould to help these set. The home-made granola recipe (page 235) that I make every weekend sometimes finds its way into these doughnuts. Guilt-free snacking at its best!

INGREDIENTS

DOUGHNUTS

200 g dark chocolate, chopped
2 tbsp almond/walnut butter
75 g granola (page 235)

TOPPING

50 g milk chocolate, melted, optional

METHOD

Place the chocolate in a glass bowl. Heat the cream till hot but not boiling and pour over the chocolate.
Allow to stand for 10–15 minutes until the chocolate softens, then stir gently until smooth. Repeat twice after every 20 minutes.
Gently whisk in the nut butter until incorporated.
Fold in the toasted granola.
Divide the mixture into the silicon mini doughnut moulds and refrigerate for a couple of hours, until set.
Demould, drizzle over with the melted chocolate.

WHAT IF?

If you want to make these vegan, you can use vegan chocolate instead.

Dark Chocolate & Berries

SMOOTHIE BOWL

✂ MAKES 1 SERVING

One of my favourite quotes is 'Put "eat chocolate" at the top of your list of things to do today. That way, at least you'll get one thing done.'

A handful of my chocolate-based recipes came around while collaborating with brands to create simple, fun content for Instagram and workshops. Devising smoothie bowls was one way to include chocolate easily in your daily routine, a guilt-free way to begin your day!

INGREDIENTS

2 ripe bananas (peeled, chopped, frozen)
5–6 strawberries, frozen
200 g mixed berries, frozen
2 tbsp cocoa powder
1 tsp beetroot powder, optional
6–8 walnut halves
1–2 tbsp nut milk
Maple syrup or honey, to taste

TOPPING

Walnut granola
Chocolate flakes
Cocoa nibs
Fresh berries

METHOD

Add the frozen fruit, cocoa powder, beetroot powder and walnuts to a heavy-duty blender. Allow to sit at room temperature for about 5 minutes to gently thaw before beginning to process.

Add the nut milk and sweetener as required. Process until very smooth and fluffy.

Use a spatula to check if all the fruit has been processed. A half-full blender jar works best.

Garnish with granola, dehydrated and fresh strawberries, chocolate, cocoa nibs, berries and fresh mint/edible flowers.

WHAT IF?

If you don't have berries, you can use two roasted beetroots instead.

Chocolate & Berries

GRANOLA PARFAITS

¶ MAKES 4 SERVINGS

There are so many ways to wake up to goodness, especially if berries are in season. If you have a jar of granola, even better. These parfaits don't take more than five minutes to layer. Also try serving them in pretty glasses . . . stem glasses are fun!

INGREDIENTS

200 ml cream
200 g Greek yogurt
2 tbsp honey
125 g dark chocolate granola
400 g mixed fresh berries

METHOD

Whisk the cream and yogurt until smooth, then whisk in the honey. Taste and adjust the sweetness.
Layer the granola, cream mix, honey, fruit . . . and repeat!

(Tip: Use a piping bag or a Ziploc bag to pipe in the cream mix to make it neat.)

Use any seasonal fruit you enjoy, for instance, make a banana strawberry parfait, black forest parfait, banoffee parfait with salted caramel.
It's a good idea to make a parfait bar and get kids to 'build their own' colourful parfaits.
Use only cream to make a dessert parfait. Alternatively, use only Greek yogurt for a lighter, slimmer version!

Whipped White Chocolate
SUMMER PARFAITS

🍴 **MAKES 4–6 SERVINGS**

I don't use white chocolate in desserts very often, but the few recipes you'll find in the book are quite rich and satisfying. This summer parfait is one such recipe. Luxurious and creamy, a little goes a long way since it's quite indulgent. I added mangoes and cherries which makes it refreshing, as well as balances the sweetness. Tart cherries and berries pair beautifully with this summer parfait too!

INGREDIENTS

200 g white chocolate, chopped fine
85 ml cream
115 g Greek yogurt

LAYERING

CHERRY COMPOTE

100 g fresh cherries, stoned
1 tbsp brown sugar
Juice of ½ a lime

1 large ripe mango, puréed
1 large ripe mango, diced
100 g fresh cherry compote

TOPPING
Fresh cherries
Diced mango
Fresh mint

METHOD

Place the chocolate in a glass bowl. Heat the cream till hot, but not boiling, and pour over the chocolate. Allow to stand for 10–15 minutes until the chocolate softens, then stir gently until smooth. Whisk in the Greek yogurt, then cover with clingwrap and refrigerate for a couple of hours.
Once firm, use an electric hand-beater and whip on high speed until smooth.
Alternatively, use a balloon whisk.

Place all the ingredients into a manual chopper and work into a rough coulis. The sugar continues to break the fruit down as it stands.

ASSEMBLE

Layer in stem glasses with fresh mango puree, fresh cherry compote, diced mangoes, etc.
Garnish with fresh cherries, mango and mint.

WHAT IF?

If you don't have stone fruit, apples and strawberries are good substitutes. Other pairings could be a mix of berries and lime curd, marmalade and strawberries, or even bittersweet chocolate and coffee.

Chocolate Banoffee
SUMMER PARFAITS

MAKES 4–6 SERVINGS

A freshly made jar of salted caramel, too many bananas on hand, and a head full of ideas led to these parfaits. They come together faster than you can imagine, and are so much easier than banoffee pie. The elements are pretty much the same, other than a layer of chocolate ganache, and of course walnuts in the biscuit base. These work so well in glasses, can be made ahead and need no fancy equipment except for a little elbow grease!

Also a great way to sneak bananas into dessert because hey, not all kids love bananas!

INGREDIENTS

BISCUIT LAYER

100 g digestive biscuits, crushed
50 g walnuts, chopped
15 g brown sugar
30 g clarified butter/ghee, melted, cooled

CHOCOLATE LAYER

80 g dark chocolate, chopped fine
125 ml cream

CREAM LAYER

150 ml cream, chilled
20 g brown sugar

TOPPING

¼ jar salted caramel sauce (page 255)
2 bananas sliced

METHOD

Place digestive biscuits, walnuts and brown sugar in a dry grinder and blend to a fine meal. Work in short pulses. Reserve ½ cup for the top layer. Add the clarified butter/ghee to the remainder and stir into the mix.

Place the chocolate in a glass bowl. Heat the cream till hot but not boiling and pour over the chocolate. Allow to stand for 10–15 minutes until the chocolate softens, then stir gently until smooth. Cool to a spreadable consistency.

Whisk together until smooth.

ASSEMBLE (IN GLASSES)

Divide the biscuit crumb and gently press down to make a base.
Spoon over the dark chocolate layer.
Top with sliced bananas.
Drizzle over 1–2 tsp of salted caramel sauce each.
Cover with the sweetened cream, dividing it between glasses.
Top with the reserved crumb mix.
Garnish with chocolate curls, shards, candied walnuts, etc.

Basics to Bottle

All the recipes under this section are eggless.

Dark Chocolate Ganache

This is a basic and versatile recipe which comes together well. As it is with working with anything chocolate in the subcontinent, it helps to take note of the season and the room temperature. Chocolate is easier to handle in winter as compared to summer or the monsoons; it just behaves differently. It may be pertinent to add that the percentage of cocoa in your choice of chocolate will define how thick or thin the ganache will turn out to be. In addition, the ratio of cream to chocolate will also determine the texture of the ganache. More cream means a softer ganache.

I'm including some tips below that have helped in my 'chocolate journey'.

TIPS

• The cream should be hot, but not boiling. Chocolate is quite sensitive to sudden changes in temperature. If the cream is too hot, it can cause the fat in the chocolate to separate.

• Make sure the chocolate is chopped fine.

• Pour the hot cream over the chopped chocolate. This allows the heat of the cream to melt the chocolate while bringing the temperature of the cream down.

• Let it rest until soft (which indicates the chocolate has melted).

• Use a double boiler if required. This is my preferred way to melt chocolate as compared to using the microwave as it gives me more control over the melting.

• Whisk gently in one direction to emulsify the chocolate. Rough handling could cause the oil to separate.

• Don't be tempted to put it into the fridge before it comes together smoothly and reaches standard room temperature.

• However, achieving standard room temperature for the chocolate in our kind of summer heat can be daunting. It may need a bit of playing around. If the weather is too warm, you might consider popping the ganache to sit in the fridge while it firms up. Remember to stir it every 30 minutes. In winter, rest the ganache on your kitchen counter for a couple of hours, stirring every so often. You will notice it becoming firmer over time as it cools down.

That said, here is my recipe with a 70% chocolate that works well for me. Since the cocoa is quite high, the ganache holds form well. Honey and butter are quite optional and add gloss to the ganache.

INGREDIENTS

200 g dark chocolate, chopped fine
300 g cream
1 tbsp honey
1 tbsp butter

METHOD

Place the chocolate in a glass bowl.

Heat the cream till hot but not boiling and pour over the chocolate. Allow to stand for 10–15 minutes until the chocolate softens, then stir gently until smooth. Whisk in the honey and butter.

Let it rest for 2–3 hours, stirring every 15–20 minutes. If the weather is too warm, refrigerate it once it's smooth and at standard room temperature.

Once the ganache reaches the desired consistency, use as required.

Note:

• The recipe can be easily doubled.

• Keeps well covered for a week in the fridge, but will get firm or stiff.

• Leave it at room temperature to reach the desired consistency, else microwave it 10 seconds at a time until the consistency is reached.

• Whisk as you desire.

This recipe is good to frost cakes, cupcakes, etc. In winter, when the unsalted butter in the chocolate solidifies faster at natural room temperature in my home, I often increase the cream by ¼ portion. This is just a guideline, so it's best to be intuitive. In general, a 2:1 chocolate to cream ratio works well for truffles or stiff piping, while a 1:1.5 chocolate to cream ratio works nicely for a glaze.

Dark Chocolate Decorations

🍴 MAKES ENOUGH FOR 1 LARGE CAKE

There are so many ways to elevate a simple-looking dessert. Chocolate garnish is an element that adds a nice touch to desserts, elevating them visually. Here are a few of my go-to toppings when I am in a hurry. They work really well in winter or cool temperatures, though tend to soften or melt in the high heat of summer if the chocolate isn't tempered. I use pre-tempered chocolate for this.

(Note: These can be made ahead and stored in an airtight box at room temperature or in the fridge depending on the natural room temperature.)

INGREDIENTS

100 g dark chocolate
Parchment paper

METHOD

Place the chocolate in a large, dry glass bowl and melt using the double-boiler method.
Alternatively, melt it in the microwave at 30-second intervals. Stir until smooth.

SHARDS

With an offset spatula (or butter knife) spread a 3 x 12 inch-long strip of parchment paper thinly with the melted chocolate.
Place another strip of parchment paper on top and roll tightly into a scroll.
Secure and put in the fridge or freezer for about 15 minutes (or until required).
Unroll over a platter and use it to top the cake.

LATTICES & PATTERNS

Put the melted chocolate into a piping bag, snip off a tiny hole with a pair of scissors, then make designs on parchment paper, either free-hand or traced over a pattern. Gently move to the fridge to set for 5–7 minutes. Use as required.

LEAVES

Wash and pat dry rose leaves. Keep the stalk on to help peel off.
Coat the underside of the leaf with melted chocolate either by gently dipping in, or using a spatula/paintbrush.
Leave to set on parchment paper in the fridge, then gently peel off the leaves.

Salted Caramel Sauce

MAKES 400 GRAMS

Spoon this over practically anything chocolate. Or anything at all! Some recipes are so simple yet so amazing that you keep going back to them over and over again. This recipe for Salted Caramel Sauce is one of them. Basic, simple, four-ingredient, indulgent and always handy.

INGREDIENTS

200 g sugar
100 g butter, diced
100 ml cream
½ tsp sea salt/pink salt

METHOD

Keep all the ingredients ready. Be careful when you work with melting sugar.

Place the sugar in a heavy-bottomed saucepan over low heat, stir a couple of times, else swirl the saucepan.

Once all the sugar has melted to an even, light golden brown, work swiftly because sugar tends to burn very fast. Immediately add the butter and simmer until the butter has melted, for a couple of minutes, stirring often. Be careful since the mixture might splatter. Now carefully drizzle in the cream, stirring constantly. The mixture will continue to bubble rapidly and splatter until the temperature settles.

Stir in the sea salt, simmer for a minute. Allow to cool a little bit, then pour into a jar, or use as desired. The sauce continues to thicken as it cools.

Refrigerate the sauce once cool. It stays good for up to two weeks in the fridge.

Notes

• Store in a lidded glass jar. Heat in the microwave briefly for 10–20 seconds before using or remove the required quantity and put into a glass jar. Place the jar in a bowl of warm/hot water depending on the weather until it softens.

• Don't let the sugar get burnt or become dark, else the salted caramel will harden and nothing can be done about it.

Easy Peanut Butter

⏍ MAKES 250 GRAMS

The day I discovered how easy it was to make peanut butter at home was the last time I ever used store-bought peanut butter. Using staple ingredients found in the Indian kitchen, I normally use Haldiram's salted, roasted peanuts to make things even easier!

Once you get making peanut butter, you could also try other nut butters. For walnut butter, lightly toast walnuts in the oven for just 10–12 minutes until fragrant. Process the warm, toasted walnuts until they begin to release their oil. Flavour it with sweetener of your choice and a pinch of sea salt. I like to add a tablespoon of jaggery powder in the end and briefly process to blend in.

INGREDIENTS

200 g salted roasted peanuts
25 ml neutral oil (light olive oil, sunflower oil, etc.)
2 tbsp honey/maple syrup

METHOD

Lightly heat the peanuts to warm in a heavy-duty wok or cast iron skillet, stirring often over low heat. Warm nuts release their oils faster for nut butters.

Place them in the jar of a food processor and process with brief pulses until you see the oil getting released, scraping down the sides often. Add the honey (as required) and oil, then process it to desired smoothness.

Transfer to a lidded jar.

Notes:

• If you like a chunky texture, reserve about ½ cup after initial pulsing, and stir through in the end before transferring to a jar.

• Keeps for a week in a lidded glass jar at room temperature. If it's warm weather, sometimes you might find some oil on the top. Stir and use.

Balsamic Strawberries or Cherries

🍴 **MAKES 300 GRAMS**

When berries are in season, this is a nice way to make them last a little longer, and a great way to give dessert an instant makeover. Balsamic vinegar when simmered with berries and sugar adds a nice depth to the berries while lending them a beautiful glaze. If you have a scraped vanilla bean shell, simmer it with the berries to add even more flavour.

INGREDIENTS

300 g strawberries, sliced (or cherries, pitted)
2–3 tbsp brown sugar
1 tbsp balsamic vinegar
½ vanilla bean, scraped (optional)

METHOD

Place all the above ingredients in a heavy-bottomed saucepan and keep over low heat, stirring often.
Strain out strawberries once softened and reserve to a bowl.
Cook down until the syrup is nice and thick, and a deep red. Pour back over the strawberries.
Allow to cool completely. Refrigerate.

(**Note:** *For cherries, follow the exact same method.*)

Simple Buttermilk Substitute

I often use cultured buttermilk while baking and you'll find it in a few recipes in the book. It's available as 'plain chaach' in the local market. If you wish to try a recipe and don't have some buttermilk on hand, here's a really simple substitute.

INGREDIENTS

150 ml milk, room temperature
1 tsp plain white vinegar (or lime juice)

METHOD

Add the vinegar to the milk and leave to stand for 5 minutes until curdled.
Use as required.

Vanilla Sugar

🍴 **MAKES 300 GRAMS**

Flavoured sugars are quite fascinating, and the one I really love is vanilla sugar. Vanilla sugar is simply regular sugar infused with vanilla beans, something I learnt from my dear friend Ulyana while visiting Moscow in the early 1990s. How something so simple could offer so much flavour was amazing!

I have jars of vanilla sugar at different stages of readiness tucked away in the back of my kitchen cupboards, and I top the jars each time I use some. You could add them to bakes as a 1:1 substitute to regular sugar, sprinkle them over cake batter or on a pie crust, even top cookies with them. Vanilla sugar is lovely to add to a no-bake dessert like pudding or panna cotta, else to flavour coffee too. Here's the simplest way to make some; an absolute no-brainer.

INGREDIENTS

2–3 halved empty/scraped vanilla bean shells (once you've scraped off the insides for something)
300 g sugar

METHOD

Place the vanilla bean shells in a glass jar with a tight-fitted lid.
Pour over the sugar to cover the beans completely. Shake well. Store in a cool place at room temperature for about 3–4 weeks. Shake the jar once in a while. Top up with sugar and vanilla bean shells as often as required.

(**Note:** *For a flavour variation, rub the sugar with the zest of a lime or an orange to get instant citrus sugar. If you have fragrant dried lavender flowers or dried mint, you can do the same, but here, place the dried flowers/ leaves in a muslin potli to infuse the sugar.*)

Vanilla Extract

Nothing better than making your own pure vanilla extract at home, and it needs just 2 ingredients. Vanilla beans, of course, and some vodka. Any standard vodka works well.

INGREDIENTS

6 vanilla beans
250 ml vodka (any standard variety)

METHOD

Take a clean glass bottle with a swing type cap or a screwtop lid.
Split the vanilla beans open and place in the bottle. Pour over the vodka (using a funnel helps).
Place the lid on tightly, then store the bottle in a cool dark place for about 4–6 months.
Give the bottle a good shake every week or so.

Fresh Pumpkin Purée

🍴 MAKES 250–275 GRAMS

I love the idea of sneaking pumpkin purée into desserts, something you'll find as you leaf through different sections of the book. Oven-roasting pumpkin gives it a nice, deep earthy sweetness. Once puréed, it pairs rather nicely with dark chocolate and a spice blend like pumpkin pie spice, cinnamon or even garam masala.

With the humble yellow pumpkin available easily all year round, pumpkin purée is rather inexpensive to make and there is a lot you can do with it. Think pie, cheesecake, pudding, tarts, smoothies, soups, truffles too!

INGREDIENTS

500 g fresh pumpkin wedge, with skin (peela kaddu)

METHOD

Wash a slice of pumpkin well and scrape off the seeds, leaving the peel on.

Wrap the slice well in aluminium foil and bake at 180°C for about 30 minutes until soft to the touch.

Spoon the softened pumpkin off the peel once warm, and blend to a smooth purée.

(**Note:** *To save time and electricity, bake the pumpkin in the oven while something else is already baking. This can be made ahead and keeps well in an airtight box in the fridge for two or three days.*)

Everyday Garam Masala

⚇ MAKE AS MUCH AS YOU LIKE!

The garam masala I add to my desserts like the fruit cake, garam masala pudding or truffles is normally the one I use in my kitchen for my stir-fries and curries. My endless supply of garam masala comes from my mum's friends who have yet to share a recipe despite several requests. They all eyeball the spice mix. I managed to get one off my friend Sonalini (who also helped me get this cookbook together). This garam masala is her mother's version.

If, however, the thought of a full-bodied garam masala scares you, my sweet friend Marryam, who has written the foreword for my book, very generously shared her version of a mild spice mix, which is as mild and gentle as she is (not to say that Sonalini's mother is not!).

SONALINI'S MOTHER'S EVERYDAY GARAM MASALA

INGREDIENTS

100 g cumin seeds/whole zeera
25 g whole pepper/gol mirch
10 green cardamom/choti elaichi
10 black cardamom/badi elaichi
20 cloves/lavang
20 g cinnamon sticks/daalchini
10 g nutmeg/javitri
10 g star anise

METHOD

Dry roast in a heavy-bottomed wok/kadhai/griddle over very low heat until fragrant. Cool completely. Grind and store in an airtight glass jar.

MARRYAM'S MILD GARAM MASALA/INDIAN PIE SPICE

INGREDIENTS

6 tsp cinnamon
3 tsp nutmeg
1 tsp green cardamom

METHOD

Sift together and store in an airtight glass jar.

Acknowledgements

To my son, who thinks I make the best desserts and take the best food pictures, and relentlessly pushes me to get better and better, up my game and constantly churn out new stuff! It's a mix of roses and brickbats from him that keeps me on my toes. My daughter, who most patiently designed the layout of the book, wanted what was best for her mum's first cookbook. This is only the second book she has ever designed, but her first cookbook design! It is exactly how I wanted my first cookbook to look. Then, of course, my better half, who is just so unbelievably patient and indulgent. My incessant banter, non-stop hoarding of props, recipe trials and endless clutter drove me quite crazy; I'm not sure how he lived through it! Also my parents, who thought I could write the book in a day—after all, I am the family baker! I couldn't have done it without their support because I am the greatest procrastinator there ever was! Thank you all.

While I never imagined I would perhaps write a cookbook someday, the idea of a chocolate book was born on a car ride in Hyderabad in 2016. It was my sweet friend Bina, who blogs at A Bit Wholesomely, who egged me on, saying that the one thing she missed was a good chocolate recipe book in India. I agreed 'wholesomely' and I am eternally grateful to her for igniting this spark!

Equally grateful to 'the girls' who've constantly rallied behind me, making me put pen to paper to write this book. This book wouldn't have happened without Sonalini, Ruchira, Parul, Anamika and Madhuli, who believed I could 'do this'. Sonalini was also my editor from the word go, quite the best thing that kept me going. Gratitude also to my sweet editor Gurveen from Penguin Random House India. Both Gurveen and Sonalini were very patient with me, knowing how distracted I can be. It's quite an art to get me to focus, and these two seem to have excelled at it!

And a huge shout-out to Marryam, who's written the foreword to my little baby book so large-heartedly, and who believes I can bake almost anything. You keep me in splits with your constant messages and tongue-in-cheek humour, Marryam— Thank you for being you!

A Word of Gratitude

Last but not least, a shout-out to a few brands, big and small, that have made my journey so worthwhile, so satisfying, and often much simpler!

Stoneware, Serveware & Glassware
Devnow (@devnow • www.urbandazzle.com)

Handcrafted Wood
Parvinder Singh Anand (@psanand81)

Creating Magic Out of Clay
A Clay Story by Anumita (@a.clay.story • www.aclaystory.com)

Bakeware
Meyer (@potsandpans • www.potsandpans.in)
Amazon Basics (www.amazon.in)

My Amazon Picks
You can find a list of my Amazon picks here. I keep adding things I find useful:
www.amazon.in/shop/passionateaboutbaking

About the Author

Deeba Rajpal's passions in life are baking, cooking, everything coffee, hoarding vintage props, food styling and photography. She has two kids, two dogs, and a better half, who are all her greatest critics (yes, the furries too) and the motivation for her culinary adventures! Travelling to old cities in India, flea markets, animals and nature are her other interests.